Björkhagen MODERN SWEDISH GRAMMAR

Modern
Swedish Grammar

by IM. BJÖRKHAGEN

Late Lecturer in Swedish in
the University of London

Ninth Edition (Revised)

SVENSKA BOKFÖRLAGET / STOCKHOLM

Norstedts

STOCKHOLM 1962. KUNGL. BOKTRYCKERIET P. A. NORSTEDT & SÖNER

Preface

My original plan was to publish a Reader and Grammar combined in one volume, but for several reasons it was found unpractical. The two parts are therefore published separately. The Reader, called *First Swedish Book*, forms a complement to the Grammar and contains practical exercises in reading, conversation, writing, etc.

For the analysis and description of the Swedish sound-system I have enjoyed the valuable assistance of Prof. Daniel Jones and Miss Lilias E. Armstrong, B.A., of the Phonetics Department, University College, London. Miss Armstrong has also kindly undertaken to read the proofs of the phonetic part of the book, for which I here beg to express my sincere thanks.

The grammatical terminology is in accordance with the recommendations of the Joint Committee on Grammatical Terminology (published by John Murray, London, 1920).

I have much pleasure in thanking Mr Sidney J. Charleston, M.A., F.R.Hist.S., late lecturer in English in the University of Upsala, Sweden, for his great kindness in revising the manuscript and proof-sheets and for the many valuable suggestions he has furnished.

Iм. Bjȫrkhagen

PREFACE TO NINTH EDITION

The ninth edition of *Modern Swedish Grammar* has been thoroughly revised and in parts re-written. The phonetic transcription has been slightly modified with a view to making it easier to read. Some grammatical rules have been given a different wording, and a number of new examples have been added. As far as possible the old numbering of sections has been retained.

The diagrams showing the Swedish sound-system and the tones have been improved with the aid of modern recording apparatus kindly placed at my disposal by Lektor Claes Christian Elert of the *Fonetiska Forskningslaboratoriet*, University of Stockholm, and I avail myself of this opportunity to express my hearty thanks for his assistance.

I. B.

Contents

TABLE OF SWEDISH CONSONANTS

| | Labial | | Dental | Post-Alveolar | Palatal | Velar | Glot |
	Bi-labial	Labio-dental					
Plosive	p b		t d	ṭ ḍ		← k g	
Nasal	(m̥) m		n	ṇ		← ŋ	
Lateral			l	ḷ			
Rolled				r			
Fricative		f v	s	ṣ	ç j		h

SWEDISH VOWELS COMPARED WITH ENGLISH VOWELS

Diagrams showing the relations of Swedish vowels to English vowels. The relative positions of the highest point of the tongue are shown by dots.

I. English vowels

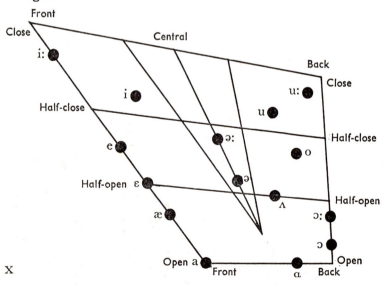

X

II. Swedish vowels

(⊙ = rounded vowel)

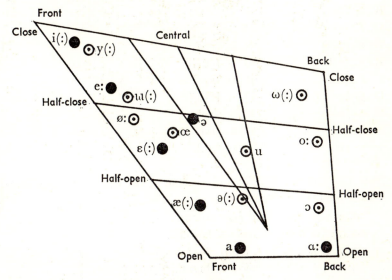

NOTE. — *a)* Length of a vowel is indicated by a colon (:). A colon in brackets indicates that the vowel occurs both long and short.

NOTE. — *b)* In Swedish the lip-articulation plays a much more important part than in English. The majority of Swedish vowels are "rounded", viz [y, ɯ, ø, œ, ə, u, ɔ, o, ω]

THE SWEDISH ALPHABET

A	a	[ɑ:]	K	k	[ko:]	U	u	[ɯ:]
B	b	[be:]	L	l	[ɛl]	V	v	[ve:]
C	c	[se:]	M	m	[ɛm]	W	w	[du'bəlt ve:]
D	d	[de:]	N	n	[ɛn]			
E	e	[e:]	O	o	[ω:]	X	x	[ɛks]
F	f	[ɛf]	P	p	[pe:]	Y	y	[y:]
G	g	[ge:]	Q	q	[kɯ:]	Z	z	[sɛ:'ta`]
H	h	[ho:]	R	r	[ær]	Å	å	[o:]
I	i	[i:]	S	s	[ɛs]	Ä	ä	[æ:]
J	j	[ji:]	T	t	[te:]	Ö	ö	[ø:]

Note that the letters *å*, *ä*, and *ö* come at the end of the alphabet. This is important when looking up a word in a dictionary.

a, o, u, å are called *hard* vowels.

e, i, y, ä, ö are called *soft* vowels.

b, d, g, j, l, m, n, r, v are *voiced* consonants.

f, h, k, p, s, t are *voiceless* (breathed) consonants.

q and *w* occur only in a few names of persons and places and are pronounced [k] and [v] respectively, e. g. *Lindquist* [li'n/d/-kvi`st, li'ŋkvi`st].

z occurs in a few words of foreign origin and is pronounced as voiceless *s*.

Pronunciation

Sounds and Phonetic Symbols

(Compare diagrams and table on pp. VIII—IX)

VOWELS   1

(1) [i]¹   Swedish short [i] is closer (i. e. the tongue is closer to the
palate) than the English *i* in 'sin'. Swedish *sin* [sin] 'his',
is pronounced like English *seen* with the vowel shortened.
Swedish long [i:]², e. g. in *bi* [bi:] 'bee', is closer than
the vowel in English 'bee'. When fully stressed it ends
with a fricative sound [j], caused by the friction between
the tongue and the palate.

EXAMPLES: *vind* [vind] 'wind'; *vi* [vi:/j/] 'we'.

(2) [y]   is pronounced with the same tongue-position as [i], but
the lips are energetically rounded and protruded. It is a
typically "rounded" vowel. The sound is similar to French
u and German *ü*, which, however, have narrower lip-
opening. Long [y:] when fully stressed often ends with a
fricative sound [j] (just as [i:]).

EXAMPLES: *synd* [synd] 'sin'; *ny* [ny:/j/] 'new'.

_____

¹ Phonetic transcriptions are placed in square brackets.
² In the phonetic transcription a colon after a vowel indicates that the vowel is
long. See § 5.

(3) [e:] is about the same sound as French *é* and German *e*. This vowel is always long [e:]. Care should be taken not to diphthongize it. The easiest way to produce it is to lengthen out the English vowel in 'lid' with tip of tongue pressed against the lower teeth, and tongue muscles tense.

EXAMPLES: *ek* [e:k][1] 'oak'; *sen* [se:n][1] 'late'.

(4) [ø:] is pronounced with practically the same tongue-position as [e:] and the same lip-position as [y:] (lips rounded and protruded). It is approximately the same sound as French *eu* in *peu* (lengthened). It only occurs long.

EXAMPLES: *dö* [dø:] 'to die'; *röd* [rø:d] 'red'.

(5) [ɯ:] is pronounced with practically the same tongue-position as [e:] and [ø:], but the lip-opening is reduced to a minimum (about the size of a pin's head). In stressed syllables the sound is always long and ends up with a bilabial fricative, caused by friction between the lips. That is the reason why English people imagine they hear a *b* or a *p* after it. When short (in unstressed syllables) it lacks the fricative.

EXAMPLES: *hus* [hɯ:s] 'house'; *musik* [mɯsi:'k] 'music'.

(6) [ɛ] is the same sound as English *e* in 'bed' (or a little closer). It occurs both long and short.

EXAMPLES: *häst* [hɛst] 'horse'; *räv* [rɛ:v] 'fox'.

(7) [œ] is pronounced with practically the same tongue-position as [ɛ], but with rounded lips. The lip-opening is wider than for [ø:] or [y]. This sound only occurs short. It is similar to French *eu* in *neuf*.

EXAMPLES: *höst* [hœst] 'autumn'; *fötter* [fœ'tər] 'feet'.

---

[1] Not [eik], [sein].

2

(8) [æ] is approximately the same sound as Southern English *a* in 'marry' (a little closer). It is used before *r*, and occurs both long and short.

EXAMPLES: *här* [hæ:r] 'here'; *Herr* [hær] 'Mr'; *värk* [værk] 'pain'.

(9) [a] only occurs short. It is like Northern English *a* in 'man' or French *a* in *la*. A Southern English speaker may produce it by isolating out the first element of the diphthong in *how* [hau] or *my* [mai], drawing the corners of the mouth somewhat to the sides (as when smiling).

EXAMPLES: *hatt* [hat] 'hat'; *man* [man] 'man'.

(10) [ə] is like English *e* in 'finger' or English *a* in 'alike', though a little closer and nearer the front-position (i. e. further forward in the mouth), especially in double-tone[1] words, where it becomes rather like [ɛ].

EXAMPLES: *finger* [fi'ŋər] 'finger'; *hatten* [ha'tən] 'the hat'; *inte* [i'ntə` *or* i'ntɛ`] 'not'.

(11) [ɑ:] is articulated a little further back than English *a* in 'father' and with slight lip rounding. This sound only occurs long.

EXAMPLES: *var* [vɑ:r] 'was'; *tala* [tɑ:'la`] 'speak'.

(12) (ɔ) is rather like the English vowel in 'clock', or in 'ought' when shortened, but has more lip rounding. It only occurs short.

EXAMPLES: *kopp* [kɔp] 'cup'; *klocka* [klɔ'ka`] 'clock'.

(13) [o:] is closer than the English vowel in 'ought' and has more lip rounding. The lip opening is narrow as for English *o* in 'do'. The sound is nearly always long.

EXAMPLES: *son* [so:n] 'son'; *två* [tvo:] 'two'.

---

[1] See § 4. In the phonetic transcription double-tone words are marked with two accents, i. e. ['] and [`]. See § 5.

(14) [ɷ] is like the English *oo* in 'book' but with much more lip rounding and an extremely narrow lip opening (as for [ɯː]). The sound occurs both long and short. When it is long and fully stressed, it ends up with a bilabial fricative, caused by friction between the lips (just as [ɯː]). That is the reason why English people imagine they hear a *b* or a *p* after it. When it is short, the lip opening is a little wider and the friction is omitted.

EXAMPLES: *bok* [bɷːk] 'book'; *hon* [hɷn] 'she'.

(15) [u] is pronounced with the highest point of the tongue further forward (nearer to the central position) and a little lower than for English *u* in 'put'. The sound resembles the first short element of the diphthong in English 'hope' as pronounced by educated Londoners. The easiest way to produce it is perhaps to aim at English *u* in 'up' while keeping the lips in the same position as for English *o* in 'do'. This sound only occurs short.

EXAMPLES: *upp* [up] 'up'; *hund* [hund] 'dog'.

(16) [ə] is a little lower than Swedish [u] in *upp* and articulated nearer to the central tongue-position. The sound is intermediate between the English vowels in 'bird' and 'up' with lip-rounding as for [œ] (the opening between the lips is a little wider than for Swedish [u] in *upp*). It is used before *r*, and occurs both long and short.

EXAMPLES: *för* [fəːr] 'for'; *dörr* [dər] 'door'.

2 CONSONANTS

Labial consonants

(produced with the lips)

The Swedish labial consonants *p*, *b*, *m*, *f*, *v* are pronounced like the English corresponding sounds.

NOTE. — (a) At the beginning of fully stressed syllables, especially before a vowel, *p* is more aspirated (i. e. pronounced with a stronger puff of breath after it) than in English.

EXAMPLES: *park* [park] 'park'; *pund* [pund] 'pound'.

NOTE. — (b) Swedish *m* is voiceless (whispered) in words ending in *-ism* or *-asm*. The lips are closed, and the breath passes through the nose without producing any sound. Phonetic symbol: [m̥].

EXAMPLES: *mekanism* [mɛkani'sm̥] 'mechanism'; *entusiasm* [aŋtɯ-sia'sm̥] 'enthusiasm'. — Note also *rytm* [rytm̥] 'rhythm'.

NOTE. — (c) The English sound represented by *w* (as in 'we') does not occur in Swedish. The letter *w* is used in many proper names but is pronounced as [v].

EXAMPLE: *Wallin* [vali:'n].

Dental consonants

(produced with the tip of the tongue against the inner edge of the upper teeth)

Swedish *t, d, n, l, s* are purely dental sounds, not alveolar as in English. (Alveolar sounds are produced with the tongue touching the rim over the roots of the upper teeth.)

NOTE. — (a) Swedish *l*, in all positions, is like English *l* in 'leave'. The main part of the tongue takes up the position of a *front* vowel, e. g. [i:]. This is the so called "clear" *l*, used in English before vowels. In the "dark" variety of English *l*, used before consonants and finally, as in 'field', 'feel', 'table', there is a raising of the *back* of the tongue. This "dark" *l* does not occur in Swedish.

EXAMPLES: *fält* [fɛlt] 'field'; *full* [ful] 'full'; *fågel* [fo:'gəl] 'bird'.

NOTE. — (b) At the beginning of fully stressed syllables, especially before a vowel, *t* is more aspirated (i. e. pronounced with a stronger puff of breath after it) than in English.

EXAMPLES: *tå* [to:] 'toe'; *tal* [tɑ:l] 'speech'; *ting* [tiŋ] 'thing'.

5

NOTE. — (c) The English th-sound, as in 'think', 'then', does not occur in Swedish.

NOTE. — (d) Swedish s is always voiceless (as in the English word 'kiss'), never voiced [z] as in 'busy'.

Post-alveolar Consonants

(produced with the tip of the tongue against the back part of the upper teeth-ridge)

The specifically post-alveolar sound in Swedish is r. It is, as a rule, faintly rolled (trilled), especially between vowels and after a consonant.

EXAMPLES: *bara* [bɑːˈraˋ] 'only'; *från* [froːn] 'from'.

In other positions it is often fricative (the air in escaping produces a friction between the tip of the tongue and the back part of the teeth-ridge).

EXAMPLES: *eller* [ɛˈlər] 'or'; *arm* [arm] 'arm'.

Retroflex consonants

When the dental sounds t, d, n, l, s are immediately preceded by r in the spelling, they become post-alveolar instead of dental, i. e. their point of articulation is moved further back, approximately to the r-position, further back than English t, d, n, l, s. The tip of the tongue is curled somewhat backwards to the back part of the teeth-ridge. The resulting sounds might be described as "retroflex" t, d, n, l, s. Phonetic symbols: [ṭ, ḍ, ṇ, ḷ, ṣ].[1] Orthographically these sounds are represented by the spellings rt, rd, rn, rl, rs. In the pronunciation the r is silent, and the following consonant acquires the retroflex character. Practise the following word pairs:

---

[1] Note the dot under the letters.

6

Dental [t, d, n, l, s]		Retroflex [ṭ, ḍ, ṇ, ḷ, ṣ]	
stat [stɑːt]	state	start [stɑːṭ]	start
bod [bɷːd]	shop	bord [bɷːḍ]	table
vana [vɑːˈnaˋ]	habit	varna [vɑːˈṇaˋ]	warn
kal [kɑːl]	bald	Karl [kɑːḷ]	Charles
mosse [mɔˈsəˋ]	bog	i morse [i mɔˈṣəˋ]	this morning

Retroflex [ṣ] resembles the English *sh*-sound in 'she', but it is formed further back. The tip of the tongue is curled back behind the ridge of the upper teeth. The lips are considerably rounded.

EXAMPLES: *först* [fəṣṭ] 'first'; *kors* [kɔṣ] 'cross'; *person* [pæṣɷːˈn] 'person'.

In groups of words, spoken without a pause between them, initial dental sounds become amalgamated with a final *r* in a preceding word to form the retroflex variety.

EXAMPLES: *för stor* [fə ṣtɷːr] 'too big'; *för tidigt* [fə ṭiːˈdit] 'too soon'; *har ni hört?* [hɑː ṇi həːṭ] 'have you heard?'; *kommer du?* [kɔˈmə ḍu] 'are you coming'?; *hur lång?* [hu: ḷɔŋ] 'how long?'; *han kommer snart* [han kɔˈmə ṣnɑːṭ] 'he will soon be here'.

Dental sounds following immediately after a retroflex sound become retroflex by attraction.

EXAMPLES: *torsdag* [tɷːˈṣda] 'Thursday'; *förstå* [fəṣtoː] 'understand'; *hur står det till?* [hu: ṣto: ḍə tiˈl] 'how are you?'; *barndom* [bɑːˈṇ-ḍɷˋm] 'childhood'; *först då* [fəṣṭ ḍoː] 'not until then'; *förslag* [fə-ṣlɑːˈg] 'suggestion'.

Retroflex [ṣ] is also used as the ordinary *sh*-sound.

EXAMPLES: *passion* [paṣɷːˈn] 'passion'; *sju* [ṣʉ:] 'seven'; *skinn* [ṣin] 'skin'; *stjärna* [ṣæːˈnaˋ] 'star'.

Palatal Consonants

(articulated by the front part of the tongue against the palate)

The voiced palatal sound [j] may be formed by pronouncing Swedish [iː] with a very narrow space between the tongue and the palate so as to produce audible friction. It resembles English *y* in 'yes' but is, as a rule, accompanied by more friction. In rapid speech it often loses its fricative character.

EXAMPLES: *ja* [jɑ:] 'yes'; *jul* [jɯ:l] 'Christmas'; *gärna* [jæ:ˈna`] 'willingly'.

The corresponding voiceless (or breathed) sound is represented by the phonetic symbol [ç]. It is articulated in the same place and manner but with breath substituted for voice. The point of articulation is a little further back than German *ch* in *ich*.

EXAMPLES: *tjock* [çɔk] 'thick'; *käpp* [çɛp] 'stick'; *kjol* [çω:l] 'skirt'.

Velar Consonants

(articulated by the back part of the tongue against the palate)

[k], [g] and [ŋ] (ng) are pronounced as in English, except in a final position, when their point of articulation is moved much further forward, so that the front of the tongue (instead of the back) touches the palate, approximately in the position for the vowels [e] or [i].

EXAMPLES: *tjock* [çɔk] 'thick'; *tack* [tak] 'thank you'; *fisk* [fisk] 'fish'; *lik* [li:k] 'like'; *stig* [sti:g] 'path'; *såg* [so:g] 'saw'; *flög* [flø:g] 'flew'; *säng* [sɛŋ] 'bed'; *lång* [lɔŋ] 'long'; *tänk* [tɛŋk] 'think'.

At the beginning of a fully stressed syllable, especially before a vowel, [k] is more aspirated than in English, i. e. it is followed by a slight puff of breath.

EXAMPLES: *ko* [kω:] 'cow'; *kust* [kust] 'coast'; *kopp* [kɔp] 'cup'.

3 LENGTH OF SOUNDS

(*a*) In Swedish a stressed syllable (principal stress or strong secondary stress, see § 10) is always *long*.

(*b*) If the vowel in a stressed syllable is long, the following consonant is short. In the phonetic transcription used in this book a colon placed immediately after a vowel indicates that the vowel is long.

EXAMPLE: *tal* [tɑ:l] 'speech' (long [ɑ:] and short [l]).

(c) If the vowel in a stressed syllable is short, the following consonant is long.

EXAMPLE: *tall* [tal] 'fir-tree' (short [a] and long [l]).

(d) A long sound (vowel or consonant) can only occur in a stressed syllable. In unstressed syllables all sounds are short.

(e) In a stressed syllable the vowel is long if it is followed by one consonant (in the spelling). The vowel is short if it is followed by more than one consonant.[1]

EXAMPLES:

Long vowel		Short vowel	
tak [tɑːk]	'roof'	tack [tak]	'thanks'
lam [lɑːm]	'lame'	lamm [lam]	'lamb'
fina [fiːˈnaˋ]	'fine' (plural)	finna [fiˈnaˋ]	'find'
mat [mɑːt]	'food'	mast [mast]	'mast'

(f) A vowel which is long in the uninflected form of a word usually remains long in inflected forms, e. g. *fin* [fiːn] 'fine', neuter form *fint* [fiːnt]; *fågel* [foːˈgəl] 'bird', plural form *fåglar* [foːˈglaˋr]; *person* [pæʂɷːˈn] 'person'; *personlig* [pæʂɷːˈnlig] 'personal'; *köpa* [çøːˈpaˋ] 'to buy', past tense *köpte* [çøːˈptəˋ], past participle *köpt* [çøːpt]; *läsa* [lɛːˈsaˋ] 'to read', past tense *läste* [lɛːˈstəˋ]. There are, however, many exceptions, e. g. *söt* [søːt] 'sweet', neuter form *sött* [sœt]; *ny* [nyː] 'new', neuter *nytt* [nyt]; *röd* [røːd], neuter *rött* [rœt]; *god* [gɷːd] 'good', neuter *gott* [gɔt]; *möta* [møːˈtaˋ] 'to meet', past tense *mötte* [mœˈtəˋ]; *lyda* [lyːˈdaˋ] 'to obey', past tense *lydde* [lyˈdəˋ]; *bo* [bɷː] 'to dwell', past tense *bodde* [bɷˈdəˋ]; *sjö* [ʂøː] 'sea', 'lake', definite form *sjön* [ʂœn]; *snö* [snøː] 'snow', def. *snön* [snœn].

Before a genitival -*s* the long vowel of a noun is sometimes shortened, e. g. *Gud* [gɷːd] 'God', *Guds ord* [guts ɷːd] 'the word of God', *gudsfruktan* [guˈtsfruˋktan] 'the fear of God'; *hav* [hɑːv] 'sea', *havsvatten* [haˈfsvaˋtən] 'sea water'; *till sjöss* [təˋ ʂœs] 'to (at, by) sea'.

---

[1] Exceptions below under (f) and (g). Retroflex [ṭ, ḍ, ṇ, ḷ, ṣ] represented in the spelling by -*rt*, -*rd*, -*rn*, -*rl*, -*rs*, count as *one* consonant respectively. (See § 2.)

(g) When a word ends in -*m* or -*n*, the length of the consonant is not always indicated in the spelling. In the following words, for instance, final -*m* or -*n* is long (after a short vowel), though only one *m* or *n* is written:

dom [dʊm] 'judgement'; *dom* [dɔm] 'they' (coll.); *som* [sɔm] 'that' (rel. pron.); *kom* [kɔm] 'came'; *hem* [hɛm] 'home'; *man*[1] [man] (def. form *mannen*) 'man'; *mun* [mun] (def. form *munnen*) 'mouth'; *hon* [hʊn] 'she'.

(h) The combination short vowel + short consonant (as in English 'hat') only occurs in unstressed syllables. Unstressed syllables are always short.

EXAMPLE: *Han har kommit hem* [han hɑr kɔmit hɛ′m] 'he has come home'.

(i) Long consonants, which are rare in English[2], are very common in Swedish. Notice particularly the long consonants between two short vowels and the combination short vowel + long consonant + short consonant.

EXAMPLES[3]:

Between two short vowels:		Short vowel + long cons. + short cons.:	
falla [fa′l:aˋ]	'to fall'	akt [ak:t]	'act'
ladda [la′d:aˋ]	'to load'	fisk [fis:k]	'fish'
gubbe [gu′b:əˋ]	'old man'	skarp [skar:p]	'sharp'
gosse [gɔ′s:əˋ]	'boy'	skaft [skaf:t]	'handle'

(j) Special care should be taken to pronounce [k], [p], and [t] *long* after a short stressed vowel. Immediately after the articulation of the vowel the speech organs (tongue or lips) are placed in position for the consonant, but the release is deferred and preceded by a short pause or stop.

EXAMPLES: *pappa* [pa′p:aˋ] 'papa'; *flicka* [fli′k:aˋ] 'girl'; *matta* [ma′t:aˋ] 'carpet'.

---

[1] Cf *man* [mɑ:n] (def. form *manen*) 'mane' (long [ɑ:] and short [n]).

[2] E. g. long [d] in *good‿dog*, long [k] in *black‿coffee*, long [t] in *night‿time*.

[3] In the phonetic transcription of these examples the length of the consonant has been indicated by a colon after it. As a rule, however, no such indication is necessary if one goes by the rule given in the third paragraph (*c*) of this section.

10

Compare Swedish long [k], [p], [t] with English short [k], [p], [t] in the following pairs of words:

Swedish long [k] [p] [t]:	English short [k] [p] [t]:
lock [lɔk:]	lock ('curl')
topp [tɔp:]	top
skepp [ʂep:]	ship
lott [lɔt:]	lot

TONES 4

There are in Swedish two principal kinds of tones (or musical accent), viz. the single tone and the double tone. Both are subject to a great number of variations according to the position of the word (in a sentence or in isolation). Only the most important cases can be treated here.

The Single Tone (Tone I)

The single tone will in this book be referred to as TONE I. In isolated words this tone is falling. If the word consists of only one syllable, e. g. *hand* [hand], the tone is the same as in the English 'hand' [⌍]. If the word consists of more than one syllable, e. g. *handen* [ha'ndən] (definite form of *hand*), the pitch of the voice is high on the stressed (first) syllable and drops to a low note on the unstressed syllable/s/. Tone I may be represented by the diagram:

handen,

where a line (straight or curved) shows the relative pitch of the stressed syllable, and a dot the pitch of an unstressed syllable. Notice that the pitch in this case drops very little or not at all on the stressed syllable; the low pitch sets in on the following unstressed syllable. In this, Tone I differs from the falling tone in English, which drops to the low level within the stressed syllable itself and remains low on the following syllables. Compare, for instance,

English: 'finger' [fi'ŋgə] and Swedish: *finger* [fi'ŋər].

11

EXAMPLES of single-tone words of more than one syllable:

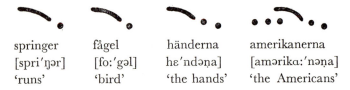

springer	fågel	händerna	amerikanerna
[spri'ŋər]	[fo:'gəl]	[hɛ'ndəŋa]	[amərikɑ:'nəŋa]
'runs'	'bird'	'the hands'	'the Americans'

The Double Tone (Tone II)

The double tone will in this book be referred to as TONE II. In double-tone words there is a double drop of the pitch, the second drop usually starting on the same note as the first, but dropping to a lower note. Tone II may be represented by the diagram:

guldring
[gu'ldri'ŋ][1]
'gold ring'

Practise by saying *guld* with Tone I, followed by *ring*, equally with Tone I (but weaker stress, see § 10 *b*). Then join the two words together, taking care not to change the tones.

EXAMPLES of double-tone words:

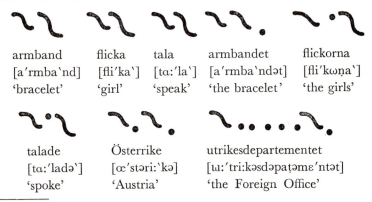

armband	flicka	tala	armbandet	flickorna
[a'rmba`nd]	[fli'ka`]	[tɑ:'la`]	[a'rmba`ndət]	[fli'kωŋa`]
'bracelet'	'girl'	'speak'	'the bracelet'	'the girls'

talade	Österrike	utrikesdepartementet
[tɑ:'ladə`]	[œ'stəri:`kə]	[ɯ:'tri:kəsdəpaṭəmɛ'ntət]
'spoke'	'Austria'	'the Foreign Office'

---

[1] The use of acute and grave accents is explained in § 5.

In the phonetic transcription used in this book, a colon [:] placed immediately after a vowel indicates that the vowel is long, e. g. *mat* [mɑ:t] 'food'. If no colon appears, the vowel is short, e. g. *matt* [mat] 'weak'.

An *acute accent* ['] placed after a vowel (in a word of more than one syllable) indicates that the tone (the pitch of the voice) begins to fall on that vowel, and that the *principal stress* (see § 10) falls on that syllable, e. g. *maten* [mɑ:'tən] 'the food'; *katten* [ka'tən] 'the cat'.

If only *one* accent is used in a word, the word is pronounced with TONE I (see § 4), e. g. *händerna* [hɛ'ndəna] 'the hands'.

TONE II (see § 4) is indicated by *two* accents, viz. an *acute accent* ['] placed after the vowel with the *principal stress*, and a *grave accent* [`] placed after the vowel with the *secondary stress* (see § 10), e. g. *guldring* [gu'ldri`ŋ] 'gold ring'; *matta* [ma'ta`] 'carpet'; *gossarna* [gɔ'saṇa`] 'the boys'.

USE OF TONE I   6

Tone I (single tone) is used:

(a) In monosyllabic words[1], e. g. *fot* [fω:t] 'foot'; *vit* [vi:t] 'white'; *gå* [go:] 'go'.

(b) In many dissyllabic words[2] ending in unstressed *-el, -en, -er*, e. g. *fågel*[3] [fo:'gəl] 'bird'; *vatten* [va'tən] 'water'; *ålder* [ɔ'ldər] 'age'; *adel* [ɑ:'dəl] 'nobility'; *handel* [ha'ndəl] 'trade'; *bibel* [bi:'bəl] 'Bible'; *ädel* [ɛ:'dəl] 'noble'; *säker* [sɛ:'kər] 'sure'; *vacker* [va'kər] 'pretty'.

EXCEPTIONS: *ängel* [ɛ'ŋə`l] 'angel'; *spegel* [spe:'gə`l] 'mirror'; *himmel* [hi'mə`l] 'heaven'; *nyckel* [ny'kə`l] 'key'; *även* [ɛ:'və`n] 'even'. These have Tone II.

---

[1] I. e. words consisting of only one syllable.
[2] I. e. words consisting of two syllables.
[3] But the plural has Tone II: *fåglar* [fo:'gla`r].

Two important groups of words ending in *-er* belong to this category, viz.:

(*1*) Most plurals of the 3rd declension (see § 65), e. g.: *fötter* [fœ'tər] 'feet'; *händer* [hɛ'ndər] 'hands'; *böcker* [bœ'kər] 'books'; *stänger* [stɛ'ŋər] 'poles'; *getter* [jɛ'tər] 'goats'; *saker* [sɑ:'kər] 'things', etc. Also: *bönder* [bœ'ndər] 'peasants'; *fäder* [fɛ:'dər] 'fathers'; *bröder* [brø:'dər] 'brothers'.

(*2*) The present singular of verbs of the 2nd and 4th conjugations (see §§ 204, 210—212), e. g.: *köper* [çø:'pər] 'buy/s/'; *vänder* [vɛ'ndər] 'turn/s/'; *binder* [bi'ndər] 'bind/s/'; *bjuder* [bjɯ:'dər] 'bid/s/'.

(*c*) In the definite forms of nouns which have Tone I in the indefinite form, e. g.: *foten* [fω:'tən] 'the foot'; *handen* [ha'ndən] 'the hand'; *fågeln* [fo:'gəln] 'the bird'; *fötterna* [fœ'təṇa] 'the feet'; *händerna* [hɛ'ndəṇa] 'the hands'; *bröderna* [brø:'dəṇa] 'the brothers'.

(*d*) In comparative forms of adjectives and adverbs having the termination *-re*[1], e. g.: *högre* [hø:'grə] 'higher'; *äldre* [ɛ'ldrə] 'older'; *mindre* [mi'ndrə] 'smaller'.

(*e*) In many names of countries, e. g.: *Sverige* [svæ'rjə] 'Sweden'; *Norge* [nɔ'rjə] 'Norway'; *England* [ɛ'ŋland]; *Tyskland* [ty'skland] 'Germany'; *Frankrike* [fra'ŋkrikə] 'France'; *Holland*; *Danmark* [da'nmark].

(*f*) In most words (except compounds) of foreign origin with the principal stress on another syllable than the first, e. g.: *artikel* [aʈi'kəl]; *student* [stɯdɛ'nt] (also in the plural: *artiklarna*, *studenterna*); *universitetet* [univæṣite:'tət] 'the university'; *piano* [piɑ:'nω]. Verbs ending in *-era*, e. g. *telefonera* [tɛləfɔne:'ra]; *fotografera* [fɔtɔgrafe:'ra].

(*g*) In verbs beginning with the prefixes *be-* or *för-*. (The simple verbs in *-a* have Tone II.) Compare:

---

[1] Comparatives ending in *-are* have Tone II. See § 7 *b)*.

14

Tone II			Tone I		
tala [tɑːˈlaˋ]	'speak'		betala [bətɑːˈla]	'pay'
hålla [hɔˈlaˋ]	'hold'		behålla [bəhɔˈla]	'keep'
följa [fœˈljaˋ]	'follow'		förfölja [fərfœˈlja]	'persecute'
söka [søːˈkaˋ]	'seek'		försöka [fəʂøːˈka]	'try'

(*h*) In adjectives ending in -*sk*, e. g.:
engelsk [ɛˈŋəlsk] 'English'; nordisk [nʊːˈdisk] 'Scandinavian'.

USE OF TONE II   7

Tone II (double tone) is used in words that do not belong to any
of the categories enumerated in the previous section. The following
groups may be distinguished:

(*a*) The majority of native polysyllabic words[1] with the principal
stress on the first syllable, e. g.:
flicka [fliˈkaˋ] 'girl'; *flickor* [fliˈkʊˋr] 'girls'; *flickorna* [fliˈkʊŋaˋ];
gosse [gɔˈsəˋ] 'boy'; *gossar* [gɔˈsaˋr] 'boys'; *gossarna* [gɔˈsaŋaˋ]; *lärare*
[læːˈrarəˋ] 'teacher'; *gammal* [gaˈmaˋl] 'old'; *gamla* [gaˈmlaˋ]
'old'; *trogen* [trʊːˈgəˋn] 'faithful'.

(*b*) Comparatives in -*are* and superlatives in -*ast*, e. g.:
trognare [trʊːˈgnarəˋ] 'more faithful'; *trognast* [trʊːˈgnaˋst] 'most
faithful'; *trognaste* [trʊːˈgnastəˋ].

(*c*) Verbs ending in -*a*[2] (also in the inflected forms), e. g.:
kalla [kaˈlaˋ] 'call' (*kallade* [kaˈladəˋ], *kallat* [kaˈlaˋt]; *kallande*
[kaˈlandəˋ]); *binda* [biˈndaˋ] 'bind' (*bundit* [buˈndiˋt], *bunden*
[buˈndəˋn]).

(*d*) The majority of compound words, e. g.:
guldring [guˈldriˋŋ] 'gold ring'; *affärsman* [afæːˈʂmaˋn] 'business
man'; *aktiebolag* [aˈktsiəbʊːˋlag] 'limited company'; *tändstickor*
[tɛˈndstiˋkʊr] 'matches'; *Stockholm* [stɔˈkhɔˋlm]; *Andersson* [aˈn-
dəʂɔˋn]; *Bergström* [bæˈrjstrœˋm]; *Österrike*[3].

---
[1] I. e. words consisting of more than one syllable.
[2] Exceptions: verbs ending in -*era*, e. g. *studera*, *telefonera*, and verbs with the prefixes *be-* or *för-*, e. g. *betala*, *förklara*, have Tone I. See § 6 *f*, *g*.
[3] Exceptions: *England*, *Tyskland*, *Holland*, *Frankrike*, *Danmark* have Tone I.

(e) Nouns ending in -inna, -essa, -ska, e. g.:

grevinna [grevi'naˋ] 'countess'; prinsessa [prinsɛ'saˋ] 'princess';
studentska [stʉdɛ'ntskaˋ] 'girl student'.

(f) Latin words ending in -or, e. g.:

doktor [dɔ'ktɔˋr] 'doctor'; professor [prɷfɛ'sɔˋr].[1]

8   TONES AND MEANING

The meaning of a word often depends on the tone. The word *anden*,
for instance, may be pronounced either with the single tone (Tone I)
or with the double tone (Tone II). If pronounced [a'ndən] (Tone I),
it means 'the duck' (definite form of *and*). If pronounced [a'ndəˋn]
(Tone II), it means 'the spirit' (definite form of *ande* [a'ndəˋ]).
Other examples:

Tone I		Tone II	
buren [bʉː'rən]	'the cage'	buren [bʉː'rəˋn]	'carried' (past part.)
slutet [slʉː'tət]	'the end'	slutet [slʉː'təˋt]	'closed' (past part.)
panter [pa'ntər]	'panther'	panter [pa'ntəˋr]	'pledges'
eder [eː'dər]	'your'	eder [eː'dəˋr]	'oaths'

9   TONE VARIATIONS IN CONNECTED SPEECH

In connected speech, unstressed words have no tone differences.
As regards stressed words, the falling tone patterns occur, as a rule,
only at the end of a complete statement, before a full stop.[2]
In the body of the sentence, stressed words generally have *rising*
tones.

Tone I may then be represented by the diagram ⌿•, and Tone
II by the diagram ⌒⌒• The dots represent unstressed words and
syllables.

---

[1] But the plural forms have Tone I and change of stress: *doktorer* [dɔktʉː'rər],
professorer [prɷfɛsɷː'rər].
[2] Questions often end with a rising tone.

EXAMPLES:

Tone I

Böckerna   ligger   på   bordet   i   salongen.
'The books are on the table in the drawing-room.'

Han satt   på golvet   och   försökte   se ut   genom fönstret.
'He sat on the floor and tried to look out at the window.'

Tone II

Sydliga   vindar   är   inte   kalla.
'Southerly winds are not cold.'

Hon sålde   moderns   dyrbara   armband   till   en   guldsmed   i   Stockholm.
'She sold her mother's valuable bracelet to a goldsmith in Stockholm.'

STRESS (Expiratory Accent)   **10**

There are in Swedish three different degrees of stress: *principal stress, strong secondary stress,* and *weak secondary stress.* These may be indicated by the figures 3, 2 and 1 respectively, placed over the vowel of the stressed syllable. Unstressed syllables may be marked by a nought [0] over the vowel.

(*a*) *Principal stress* [3] normally falls on the first syllable of a word, e. g.: *hånden* [ha′ndən] 'the hand'; *bågare* [bɑ:′garə`] 'baker'; *guldring* [gu′ldri`ŋ] 'gold ring'; *flicka* [fli′ka`] 'girl'; *flickorna* [fli′-kωna`] 'the girls'; *kålla* [ka′la`] 'call'; *kållande* [ka′landə`] 'calling'.

17

In most words beginning with the prefix *be-* or *för-* the principal stress falls on the second syllable, e. g.:

beslŭt [bəslɯː't] 'decision'; *beslŭta* [bəslɯː'ta] 'decide'; *förbŭd* [fərbɯː'd] 'prohibition'; *förbjŭda* [fərbjɯː'da] 'forbid'.

Verbs ending in *-era* have the principal stress on *-e-*, e. g.:

studĕra [stɯde:'ra] 'study'; *telefonĕra* [tɛləfɔne:'ra] 'telephone'.

In words of French origin the principal stress generally falls on the last syllable. Also in nouns ending in *-eri* and *-ori*, e. g.:

generăl [jɛnəraː'l] 'general'; *agĕnt* [ajɛ'nt] 'agent'; *protestănt* [prɔtəsta'nt]; *natiŏn* [natsɯː'n]; *missiŏn* [misɯː'n]; *nationĕll* [natsɯnɛ'l] 'national'; *universitĕt* [univæṣite:'t] 'university'; *konditorĭ* [kɔnditɯri:'] 'confectioner's shop'; *bagerĭ* [baːgəri:'] 'bakery'.

(*b*) *Strong secondary stress* [2] in combination with Tone II (see § 4—7) falls on the second part of a compound word, e. g.:

guldrĭng; flicksköla [fli'kskɯːˋla] 'girls' school'; *universitetsprofĕssor* [univæṣite:'tsprɯfɛˋsɔr] 'university professor'.

Strong secondary stress (in combination with Tone II) falls on the suffixes *-dom, -het, -lek, -skap, -sam* and others, e. g.:

ungdŏm [u'ŋdɯˋm] 'youth'; *skönhĕt* [ṣøː'nheːˋt] 'beauty'; *kärlĕk* [çæː'leːˋk] 'love'; *vänskăp* [vɛ'nskaːˋp] 'friendship'; *underbăr* [u'ndərbaːˋr] 'wonderful'; *arbetsăm* [a'rbetsaˋm] 'hard-working'.

(*c*) *Weak secondary stress* [1] falls on the second syllable of double tone dissyllabic words (other than compounds), e. g.:

gossĕ [gɔ'səˋ] 'boy'; *gossăr* [gɔ'saˋr] 'boys'.

When several weak syllables follow in succession, weak secondary stress falls on every other syllable, counting from the syllable with the principal stress. This applies to words with Tone I as well as to words with Tone II, e. g.:

händernă [hɛ'ndəna] 'the hands'; *universitetet* [univæṣite:'tət] 'the university'; *gossarnă* [gɔ'saṇaˋ] 'the boys'; *kalladĕ* [ka'ladəˋ] 'called'.

18

(*d*) *Lack of stress* [0] occurs particularly in the second syllable of dissyllabic words with Tone I, and, alternating with weak secondary stress [1], in polysyllabic words, e. g.:

handⁿen [haˈndən]; *händⁿerna* [hɛˈndəɳa]; *gossⁿarna* [gɔˈsaɳaˋ]; *unⁱversⁱtetet.*

COLLOQUIAL FORMS   11

In colloquial Swedish there are many divergences from the written (literary) language, both as regards form and pronunciation. The following are the most important points.

(*1*) All nouns end in -*a* in the definite plural.

    EXAMPLES: *ögonen > ögona* [øːˈgɔnaˋ] 'the eyes'; *husen > husena* [huːˈsəna] 'the houses'; *barnen > barna* [baːˈɳa] 'the children'.

(*2*) The noun *huvud* [huːˈvuˋd] 'head' has the colloquial form *huve* [huːˈvəˋ] (def. form *huvet*), plural *huven* [huːˈvəˋn] (def. plur. *huvena* [huːˈvənaˋ].

(*3*) Adjectives ending in -*ig* often drop the *g*.

    EXAMPLES: *tråki/g/* [troːˈkiˋ] 'dull', *tråki/g/t, tråki/g/a.*

(*4*) Many pronouns have special colloquial forms.

    EXAMPLES: *jag* [jɑːg] is pronounced [jɑː], unstressed [ja]; *mig* [miːg], *dig* [diːg], *sig* [siːg] are pronounced [mɛj, dɛj, sɛj]; *de* [deː] and *dem* [dɛm] are both pronounced [dɔm], e. g. *de* [dɔm] *kom inte* 'they didn't come'; *tag dem!* [tɑː dɔm] 'take them!';
något [noːˈgɔˋt] and *intet* [iˈntəˋt] have the forms *någe* [noːˈgəˋ], *inge/t/* [iˈŋəˋ]; *någon* [noːˈgɔˋn] is often contracted to [nɔn]: *någonting* [nɔntiŋ], *någonsin* [nɔˈnsiˋn] 'ever'.

(*5*) The mark of the infinitive *att* [at] is sometimes pronounced [ɔ].

(*6*) In all verbs the plural forms are replaced by the singular. (This practice is also gaining ground in the written language.)

    EXAMPLES: *vi köpa > vi köper* 'we buy'; *de springa > dom springer* 'they run'; *de kunna > dom kan* 'they can'; *de sprungo > dom sprang* 'they ran'.

19

(7) The past tense of the 1st conjugation has the same form as the infinitive.

EXAMPLES: *jag kastade* > *kasta'* [ka'sta`] 'I threw'; *vi ropade* > *ropa'* [rω:'pa`] 'we shouted'.

(8) The irregular past forms *lade* [lɑ:'də`] 'laid' and *sade* [sɑ:'də`] 'said' are shortened to *la'* [lɑ:], *sa'* [sɑ:].

(9) The verb *säga* [sɛ:'ga`] 'say' is pronounced [sɛ'ja`] (present form *säger* [sɛ'jər]).

(10) A few verbs have short colloquial forms in the infinitive and the present.

EXAMPLES:

bliva, bliver > bli, blir [bli:, bli:r]	'become';
taga, tager > ta, tar [tɑ:, tɑ:r]	'take';
bedja, beder > be, ber [be:, be:r]	'request'; 'ask'; 'pray';
giva, giver > ge, ger [je:, je:r]	'give'.

(11) The following auxiliary verbs have special colloquial forms:

/jag/	är	is pronounced	[ja ɛ:]
/de/	är/o/	» »	[dɔm ɛ:]
/jag/	var	» »	[ja vɑ:]
/jag/	skall	» »	[ja ska: (ska)]
/vi/	skola	» »	[vi ska: (ska)]

(12) *Med* [me:d] 'with' is pronounced [me:];
till [til] 'to', and *och* [ɔk] 'and', in unstressed positions are pronounced [tə], [ɔ], e. g. *Ja/g/ ska/ll/ resa in till* [tə] *sta/de/n o/ch/ handla. Ska du följa me/d/?*

(13) Final *d*, *g* and *t* are often dropped after a vowel.

EXAMPLES: *det* [de:] (definite article and pronoun); *jag vet det* [ja ve:t de:]; *vad är det för dag i dag?* [va ɛ: dɛ fə ɖɑ: i dɑ:]; *hur många dagar tar det?* [hɯ:r mɔŋa dɑ:r tɑ: ɖɛ]; *god morgon* [gω mɔ'rɔ`n]; *bröd* [brø:] (definite form *brö't*, plural *brön*); *vad sade de?* [va sɑ: dɔm]; *staden* [stɑ:n] 'the town'.

(14) Final *nd* is often assimilated to *nn*.

EXAMPLES: *vind* [vin] 'wind' (also in the definite form *vinden* [vin]); *hund* 'dog', and def. form *hunden* are both pronounced [hun].

20

Key-words for the Pronunciation

VOWELS

[i:]	vi	we	[a]	hand	hand	
[i]	ring	ring	[ɑ:]	glad	glad	
[y:]	ny	new (non-neuter)	[ɔ]	boll	ball	
[y]	nytt	new (neuter)	[o:]	gå	go	
[e:]	se	see	[ω:]	god	good	
[ø:]	snö	snow	[ω]	ost	cheese	
[ɯ:]	hus	house	[u]	full	full	
[ɛ:]	väg	way	[ɵ:]	smör	butter	
[ɛ]	häst	horse	[ɵ]	mörk	dark	
[œ]	höst	autumn	[ə]	vinter	winter	
[æ:]	här	here				
[æ]	Herr	Mr				

CONSONANTS

[ŋ]	finger	[fi'ŋər]	finger
[ç]	kind	[çind]	cheek

Post-alveolar				(Dental)		
[ḍ]	bord	[bω:ḍ]	table	(bod	[bω:d]	shop)
[ṭ]	start	[stɑ:ṭ]	start	(stat	[stɑ:t]	state)
[ṣ]	i morse	[i mɔ'ṣə`]	this morning	(mosse	[mɔ'sə`]	bog)
[ṣ]	sjö	[ṣø:]	sea, lake			
[ḷ]	Karl	[kɑ:ḷ]	Charles	(kal	[kɑ:l]	bald)
[ṇ]	varna	[vɑ:'ṇa`]	warn	(vana	[vɑ:'na`]	habit)

No key-words are required for the other consonants.

Sounds and Spelling

13 VOWELS

a

The Swedish letter *a* is pronounced:

(*a*) as long [ɑː].

EXAMPLES: *ja* [jɑː] 'yes'; *dag* [dɑːg] 'day'; *bara* [bɑːˈraˋ] 'only'.

(*b*) as short [a].

EXAMPLES: *katt* [kat] 'cat'; *flicka* [fliˈkaˋ] 'girl'; *packa* [paˈkaˋ] 'to pack'; *paraply* [paraplyː] 'umbrella'.

NOTE. — Swedish short *a* in unstressed positions is never pronounced as the neutral murmur vowel [ə] heard in English words like 'address', 'America', 'Christina'. Compare English [ədreˈs, əmeˈrikə, kristiːˈnə] and Swedish [adrɛˈs, ameːˈrika, kristiːˈnaˋ].

e

is pronounced:

(*a*) as long [eː].[1]

EXAMPLES: *se* [seː] 'to see'; *lek* [leːk] 'play'; *genast* [jeːˈnaˋst] 'immediately'; *mer* [meːr] 'more'. *Erik* [eːˈrik] 'Eric'.

NOTE. — The prefix *er-* is usually pronounced [æːr].

EXAMPLES: *erkänna* [æːˈrɕɛˋna] 'to confess'; *erinra* [æːˈriˋnra] 'to remind'.

(*b*) as short (and not followed by -*r*) [ɛ].

EXAMPLES: *mest* [mɛst] 'most'; *penna* [pɛˈnaˋ] 'pencil'.

(*c*) as short and followed by -*r* [æ].

EXAMPLES: *herr* [hær] 'Mr'; *Sverige* [svæˈrjə] 'Sweden'; *berg* [bærj] 'mountain'.

---

[1] Not diphthongized [ei]!

(*d*) as the murmur vowel [ə] in unaccented syllables ending in
-*e*, -*el*, -*en*, -*er*, in the definite terminal article -*en*, -*et*, and in
the prefix *be*-.

EXAMPLES: *gosse* [gɔ'sə`] 'boy'; *handen* [ha'ndən] 'the hand';
huset [huː'sət] 'the house'; *fågel* [foː'gəl] 'bird'; *vapen* [vɑː'pən]
'weapon'; *finger* [fi'ŋər] 'finger'; *händer* [hɛ'ndər] 'hands';
betala [bətɑː'la] 'to pay'.

i

is pronounced:

(*a*) as long [iː] (close and with slight friction).

EXAMPLES: *vi* [viː] 'we'; *vis* [viːs] 'wise'; *rida* [riː'da`] 'ride';
bageri [bɑːgəri'] 'bakery'.

(*b*) as short [i].

EXAMPLES: *vind* [vind] 'wind'; *viss* [vis] 'certain'; *riddare* [ri'darə`]
'knight'; *binda* [bi'nda`] 'to bind'.

o

represents three different sounds, viz. [ω], [oː] and [ɔ]; [ω] can
occur long or short; [oː] only long; [ɔ] only short:

(*a*) long [ωː] (very close and with slight labial friction).

EXAMPLES: *sko* [skωː] 'shoe'; *mor* [mωːr] 'mother'; *mot* [mωːt]
'against'; *ord* [ωːɖ] 'word'; *borde* [bωː'ɖə`] 'ought to'; *torn*
[tωːn̩] 'tower'; *stort* [stωːt] 'large'; *olycklig* [ωː'ly`klig] 'un-
happy'; *omöjlig* [ωː'mœ`jlig] 'impossible'; *mission* [misω̩ː'n];
nation [natsω̩ː'n] (and others in -*ion*).

(*b*) short [ω].

EXAMPLES: *orm* [ωrm] 'snake'; *ost* [ωst] 'cheese'; *ond* [ωnd]
'angry'; *blomma* [blω'ma`] 'flower'; *bonde* [bω'ndə`] 'peasant'.

The plural endings -*or* (1st declension of nouns) and -*o* (past
tense of strong verbs) have short [ω].

EXAMPLES: *flickor* [fli'kω`r][1] 'girls'; *gator* [gɑː'tω`r][1] 'streets';
skrevo [skreː'vω`] 'wrote'; *kommo* [kɔ'mω`] 'came'.

---

[1] Many Swedes pronounce the plural ending -*or* as [ər]: [fli'kə`r], [gɑː'tə`r].

23

(c) long [o:] (not diphthongized [ou]!).

EXAMPLES: *son* [so:n] 'son'; *kol* [ko:l] 'coal'; *lova* [lo:'va`] 'to promise'; *sova* [so:'va`] 'to sleep'; *ordna* [o:'dna`] 'arrange'; *villkor* [vi'lko:`r] 'condition'.

Long [o:] also occurs in many words of foreign origin, e. g. *filosof* [filɔso:'f] 'philosopher'; *epok* [ɛpo:'k] 'epoch'; *mikroskop* [mikrɔsko:'p]; *dialog* [dialo:'g].

(d) short [ɔ].

EXAMPLES: *komma* [kɔ'ma`] 'to come'; *somliga* [sɔ'mliga`] 'some'; *Stockholm* [stɔ'khɔ`lm]; *bort* [bɔt] 'away'[1]; *norr* [nɔr] 'north'.

The suffixes *-or* (in Latin words) and *-on* have [ɔ], e. g. *professor* [prɷfɛ'sɔ`r][2]; *doktor* [dɔ'ktɔ`r][2]; *tretton* [trɛ'tɔ`n] 'thirteen'; *päron* [pæ:'rɔ`n] 'pear'.

NOTE. — The suffixes *-tion*, *-sion*, *-jon* (of Latin or French origin) have long [ω:], e. g. *nation* [natʂω:'n]; *mission* [miʂω:'n]; *bataljon* [bataljω:'n].

u

represents two different sounds:

(a) long [ɯ:].

EXAMPLES: *hus* [hɯ:s] 'house'; *djur* [jɯ:r] 'animal'; *sju* [ʂɯ:] 'seven'; *ful* [fɯ:l] 'ugly'; *stuga* [stɯ:'ga`] 'cottage'.

NOTE. — In the unstressed position this [ɯ] is shortened, becomes more open and loses its friction, e. g. *musik* [mɯsi:'k] 'music'; *butelj* [bɯtɛ'lj] 'bottle'; *om du kan* [ɔm dɯ kan] 'if you can'.

(b) short [u].

EXAMPLES: *hund* [hund] 'dog'; *mun* [mun] 'mouth'; *full* [ful] 'full'; *kunna* [ku'na`] 'to be able'; *gubbe* [gu'bə`] 'old man'; *kung* [kuŋ] 'king'.

---

[1] Cf. *bort* [bω:t], supine of *böra* 'ought to'.
[2] But in the plural [prɷfɛsω:'rər, dɔktω:'rər].

y

(*a*) Long [y:] (close and with friction).

EXAMPLES: *ny* [ny:] 'new'; *fyra* [fy:ˈraˋ] 'four'; *lysa* [ly:ˈsaˋ] 'to shine'.

(*b*) Short [y] (more open and without friction).

EXAMPLES: *nytt* [nyt] 'new' (neuter form); *syster* [syˈstəˋr] 'sister'; *skydda* [s̩yˈdaˋ] 'to protect'.

å

(*a*) Long [o:].[1]

EXAMPLES: *gå* [go:] 'to go'; *år* [o:r] 'year'; *låna* [lo:ˈnaˋ] 'to borrow'.

In the unstressed position this [o:] becomes more open (more like [ɔ]), e. g. *gå bort* [go bɔˈt̩] 'go away'; *på landet* [pɔ laˈndət] 'in the country'.

(*b*) short [ɔ].

EXAMPLES: *mått* [mɔt] 'measure'; *åtta* [ɔˈtaˋ] 'eight'; *lång* [lɔŋ] 'long'; *ålder* [ɔˈldər] 'age'.

ä

represents two different sounds, viz. [æ] when it is followed by *-r*, and [ɛ] in other cases. Each sound occurs both long and short.

(*a*) Long and short [æ] (followed by *-r*).

EXAMPLES:

(long [æ:]) *här* [hæ:r] 'here'; *lära* [læ:ˈraˋ] 'to learn'; *järn* [jæ:ṇ] 'iron'; *värld* [væ:d̩] 'world'; *pärla* [pæ:ˈḷaˋ] 'pearl';

(short [æ]) *värk* [værk] 'pain'; *märka* [mæˈrkaˋ] 'to mark'; *hjärta* [jæˈt̩aˋ] 'heart'.

(*b*) Long and short [ɛ] (not followed by *-r*).

EXAMPLES:

(long [ɛ:]) *nät* [nɛ:t] 'net'; *äta* [ɛ:ˈtaˋ] 'to eat'; *läsa* [lɛ:ˈsaˋ] 'to read'; *läkare* [lɛ:ˈkarəˋ] 'doctor';

(short [ɛ]) *bäst* [bɛst] 'best'; *rädd* [rɛd] 'afraid'; *äpple* [ɛˈpləˋ] 'apple'; *smälta* [smɛˈltaˋ] 'to melt'.

---

[1] Not diphthongized [ou]!

ö

represents three different sounds: [ə], [ø] and [œ].

(a) When followed by -r it represents [ə]. This sound occurs both long and short.

EXAMPLES:

(long [ə:]) *för* [fə:r] 'for'; *höra* [hə:'ra`] 'to hear'; *öra* [ə:'ra`] 'ear'; *hört* [hə:t] 'heard'; *hörn* [hə:ŋ] 'corner'; *börd* [bə:d̦] 'birth'; (short [ə]) *dörr* [dər] 'door'; *först* [fəṣt] 'first'; *mörk* [mərk] 'dark'; *större* [stə'rə] 'larger'.

(b) When not followed by -r it represents:

(1) the long vowel [ø:].

EXAMPLES: *dö* [dø:] 'to die'; *röd* [rø:d] 'red'; *öga* [ø:'ga`] 'eye'.

(2) the short vowel [œ].

EXAMPLES: *höst* [hœst] 'autumn'; *drömma* [drœ'ma`] 'to dream'; *fötter* [fœ'tər] 'feet'.

14 CONSONANTS

c

(a) In native Swedish words *c* is nearly always found in combination with *k*: *ck*, which is pronounced as long [k].
EXAMPLES: *tjock* [çɔk] 'thick'; *flicka* [fli'ka`] 'girl'.

(b) Before the 'soft' vowels *e*, *i* and *y* in words of foreign origin *c* is pronounced [s].
EXAMPLES: *cigarr* [siga'r]; *cylinder* [syli'ndər]; *cell* [sel].

(c) The combination *ch* in words of foreign (French) origin is pronounced [ṣ].
EXAMPLES: *choklad* [ṣɔkla:'d] 'chocolate'; *chef* [ṣe:f]; *chaufför* [ṣɔfə:'r] 'driver'; *charm* [ṣarm].

(d) The word *och* 'and', is pronounced [ɔk], coll. [ɔ].

26

d

(*a*) Before (a genitival) *s* the *d* is often pronounced as [t].

EXAMPLES: *Guds ord* [guts ω:d̦] 'the word of God'; *gods* [gωts] 'goods'.

(*b*) In the combination *dj* at the beginning of a syllable the *d* is mute.

EXAMPLES: *djup* [jɯ:p] 'deep'; *djur* [jɯ:r] 'animal'; *djärv* [jærv] 'bold'; *djävul* [jɛ:'vuˋl] 'devil'.

g

has several sound values.

I. It is pronounced as [g]:

(*a*) before the 'hard' vowels (*a, o, u, å*) and before a consonant.

EXAMPLES: *gata* [gɑ:'taˋ] 'street'; *god* [gω:d] 'good'; *gud* [gɯ:d] 'god'; *gå* [go:] 'go'; *saga* [sɑ:'gaˋ] 'fairy tale'; *helgon* [hɛ'lgɔˋn] 'saint'; *glad* [glɑ:d] 'glad'; *gnaga* [gnɑ:'gaˋ] 'to gnaw'; *gnida* [gni:'daˋ] 'to rub'; *gräs* [grɛ:s] 'grass'; *fåglar* [fo:'glaˋr] 'birds'.

(*b*) before *e* in unstressed syllables. (Exceptions see below under II b.)

EXAMPLES: *mage* [mɑ:'gəˋ] 'stomach'; *mager* [mɑ:'gər] 'lean'; *fågel* [fo:'gəl] 'bird'; *regel* [re:'gəl] 'rule'; *trogen* [trω:'gəˋn] 'faithful'.

(*c*) at the end of a syllable after a vowel.

EXAMPLES: *lag* [lɑ:g] 'law'; *såg* [so:g] 'saw'; *väg* [vɛ:g] 'way'.

II. It is pronounced as [j]:

(*a*) before a stressed 'soft' vowel[1] (*e, i, y, ä, ö*).

EXAMPLES: *genast* [je:'naˋst] 'immediately'; *gick* [jik] 'went'; *magister* [maji'stər] 'teacher'; *gynna* [jy'naˋ] 'to favour'; *gärna* [jæ:'ṇaˋ] 'willingly'; *göra* [jə:'raˋ] 'to make'.

---

[1] In loan-words ending in -*logi*, e. g. *zoologi*, the *g* is pronounced [g]: [sωɔlɔgi:ˋ].

(b) after *l* and *r* in the following words (and a few others):

talg [talj] 'tallow'; *helg* [hɛlj] 'church festival'; *arg* [arj] 'angry'; *varg* [varj] 'wolf'; *berg* [bærj] 'mountain'; *färg* [færj] 'colour'; *korg* [kɔrj] 'basket'; *sorg* [sɔrj] 'sorrow'; *orgel* [ɔ'rjə'l] 'organ'; *Sverige* [svæ'rjə] 'Sweden'; *Norge* [nɔ'rjə] 'Norway'.

(c) In the prefix *ge-* in words of German origin.

EXAMPLES: *gestalt* [jəsta'lt] 'figure'; *gemensam* [jəme:'nsam] 'common'.

III. It is often pronounced as [k] before *s* and *t* in the same syllable.

EXAMPLES: *högst* [hœkst] 'highest'; *högt* [hœkt] 'high' (neuter form); *dagsljus* [da'ksjɯ:ˋs] 'daylight'; *skogsfågel* [skɷ'ksfo:ˋgəl] 'forest bird'; the past participles *bragt* [brakt] 'brought', *lagt* [lakt] 'laid', *sagt* [sakt] 'said'.

IV. It is pronounced as [ŋ] before *n* in the stem of a word.

EXAMPLES: *vagn* [vaŋn] 'carriage'; *regn* [rɛŋn] 'rain'; *regna* [rɛ'ŋnaˋ] 'to rain'; *lugn* [luŋn] 'calm'; *ugn* [uŋn] 'oven'. Also in the inflected forms: *vagnen* [va'ŋnən], *vagnar* [va'ŋnaˋr]; [rɛ'ŋnət], etc.

V. It is pronounced as [ʂ] before *e* and *i* in words of French origin.

EXAMPLES: *tragedi* [traʂədi:'] 'tragedy'; *generad* [ʂəne:'rad] 'embarrassed'; *geni* [ʂəni:'] 'genius'; *ingenjör* [inʂənjə:'r] 'engineer'; *passagerare* [pasaʂe:'rarəˋ] 'passenger'; *Eugen* [eɯʂe:'n] 'Eugene'.

VI. In the combination *gj* the *g* is mute in the following words: *gjorde* [jɷ:'ḍəˋ] 'did'; *gjort* [jɷ:ṭ], *gjord* [jɷ:ḍ] 'done'; *gjuta* [jɯ:'taˋ] 'cast'.

h

is mute in the combination *hj* at the beginning of a word.

EXAMPLES: *hjul* [jɯ:l] 'wheel'; *hjälpa* [jɛ'lpaˋ] 'to help'; *hjort* [jɷ:ṭ] 'deer'; *hjärta* [jæ'ṭaˋ] 'heart'.

j

is pronounced:

(a) as [j] in most cases.

EXAMPLES: *ja* [jɑ:] 'yes'; *järn* [jæ:ɳ] 'iron'; *jul* [jɯ:l] 'Christmas'; *björn* [bjə:ɳ] 'bear'; *björk* [bjərk] 'birch'.

(b) as [ṣ] in a few words of French origin.

EXAMPLES: *journal* [ṣɯɳɑ:'l]; *projekt* [prɯṣɛ'kt]; *jackett* [ṣakɛ't] 'morning-coat'.

k

has two sound values: [k] and [ç].

I. It is pronounced as [k]:

(a) before the "hard" vowels (*a, o, u, å*).

EXAMPLES: *kall* [kal] 'cold'; *ko* [kω:] 'cow'; *kust* [kust] 'coast'; *kopp* [kɔp] 'cup'; *kål* [ko:l] 'cabbage'.

(b) before *e* and *i* in unstressed syllables.

EXAMPLES: *vacker* [va'kər] 'beautiful'; *rike* [ri:'kəˋ] 'kingdom'; *buske* [bus'kəˋ] 'bush'; *tråkig* [tro:'kiˋg] 'dull'.

(c) before or after a consonant in the same syllable.

EXAMPLES: *kniv* [kni:v] 'knife'; *krage* [krɑ:'gəˋ] 'collar'; *skåp* [sko:p] 'cupboard'; *makt* [makt] 'power'.

(d) at the end of a word (when [k] becomes palatalized).

EXAMPLES: *bok* [bω:k] 'book'; *tjock* [çɔk] 'thick'; *mask* [mask] 'worm'; *fisk* [fisk] 'fish'.

(e) before a 'soft' vowel in a few loan-words.

EXAMPLES: *jackett* [ṣakɛ't] 'morning-coat'; *monarki* [mωnarki:'] 'monarchy'; *kö* [kø:] 'queue'; *kör* [kə:r] 'choir'.

II. It is pronounced as [ç]:

(a) before the 'soft' vowels (*e, i, y, ä, ö*).

EXAMPLES: *kedja* [çe:'djaˋ] 'chain'; *kemi* [çɛmi:'] 'chemistry'; *kines* [çine:'s] 'Chinese'; *kind* [çind] 'cheek'; *kyrka* [çy'rkaˋ]

2*—616129. *Björkhagen, Modern Swedish Grammar. 9 u.*   29 'church'; *kär* [çæ:r] 'dear'; *köpa* [çø:ˈpaˋ] 'buy'; *köra* [çθ:ˈraˋ] 'drive'.

(*b*) in the combination *kj* (where *j* is mute).

EXAMPLE: *kjol* [çω:l] 'skirt'.

l

is mute in the combination *lj* at the beginning of a word.

EXAMPLES: *ljud* [jɯ:d] 'sound'; *oljud* [ω:ˈjɯ:ˋd] 'noise'; *ljus* [jɯ:s] 'light'; *ljum* [jum] 'luke-warm'; *ljuv* [jɯ:v] 'sweet'; *ljuga* [jɯ:ˈgaˋ] 'to tell lies'.

It is also mute in the words *värld* [væ:ḍ] 'world', and *karl* [kɑ:r] 'man', def. form *karl/e/n* [kɑ:ṇ].

n

is pronounced [ŋ] when it stands before *k*, and in a few words borrowed from French.

EXAMPLES: *tänka* [tɛˈŋkaˋ] 'to think'; *bank* [baŋk] 'bank'; *ankare* [aˈŋkarə] 'anchor'; *annons* [anɔˈŋs] 'advertisement'; *pension* [paŋʂω:ˈn].

The combination *ng* is pronounced [ŋ].

EXAMPLES: *lång* [lɔŋ] 'long'; *längre* [lɛˈŋrə] 'longer'; *engelsk* [ɛˈŋəlsk] 'English'; *ängel* [ɛˈŋəˋl] 'angel'; *finger* [fiˈŋər] 'finger'.

NOTE. — The [ŋ]-sound is *not* followed by a [g]-sound as in the English words *longer, finger, English* [lɔˈŋgə, fiˈŋgə, iˈŋgliʃ].

r

On the pronunciation of *r* and its effect on a following *d, l, n, s, t,* see § 2 (Retroflex consonants).

NOTE. — At the end of words Swedish *r* is not mute or changed into a murmur vowel [ə] as in English.

EXAMPLES: *finger* [fiˈŋər]; *doktor* [dɔˈktɔˋr]; *ner* [ne:r] 'down'; *gör* [jθ:r] 'does'; *far* [fɑ:r] 'father'; *mor* [mω:r] 'mother'; *här* [hæ:r] 'here'; *där* [dæ:r] 'there'; *djur* [jɯ:r] 'animal'.

30

s

is always voiceless [s] (never voiced [z]).

EXAMPLES: *svensk* [svɛnsk] 'Swedish'; *svår* [svoːr] 'difficult'; *observera* [ɔbsærveːˈra] 'to observe'; *brasa* [brɑːˈsaˋ] 'fire'.

In words ending in -/s/sion the combination -/s/si is pronounced [ʂ].
EXAMPLES: *passion* [paʂωːˈn]; *pension* [paŋʂωːˈn].

The combinations *sch, sj, skj,* and *stj* are pronounced [ʂ].

EXAMPLES: *schack* [ʂak] 'chess'; *schema* [ʂeːˈma] 'time-table'; *sju* [ʂɯː] 'seven'; *sjö* [ʂøː] 'lake'; *själ* [ʂɛːl] 'soul'; *sjätte* [ʂɛˈtəˋ] 'sixth'; *skjorta* [ʂωːˈʈaˋ] 'shirt'; *skjuta* [ʂɯːˈtaˋ] 'to shoot'; *stjäla* [ʂɛːˈlaˋ] 'to steal'; *stjärna* [ʂæːˈɳaˋ] 'star'.

The combination *sc* is pronounced [s] in *scen* [seːn] 'scene'.

The combination *sk* has two sound values: [ʂ] and [sk].

(*a*) [ʂ] before stressed "soft" vowels (*e, i, y, ä, ö*).

EXAMPLES: *sked* [ʂeːd] 'spoon'; *skinn* [ʂin] 'skin'; *skina* [ʂiːˈnaˋ] 'to shine'; *maskin* [maʂiːˈn] 'engine'; *skynda* [ʂyˈndaˋ] 'to hurry'; *skära* [ʂæːˈraˋ] 'to cut'; *skönhet* [ʂøːˈnheːˋt] 'beauty'. (Exception: *skiss* [skis] 'sketch'.)

(*b*) [sk] in other cases, i. e. before "hard" vowels (*a, o, u, å*), at the end of a root-syllable, before consonants, and before unstressed vowels.

EXAMPLES: *skaka* [skɑːˈkaˋ] 'to shake'; *skog* [skωːg] 'forest'; *skur* [skɯːr] 'shower'; *skulle* [skuˈləˋ] 'should'; *skåp* [skoːp] 'cupboard'; *fisk* [fisk] 'fish'; *färsk* [fæʂk] 'fresh'; *handske* [haˈn-skəˋ][1] 'glove'; *fisken* [fiˈskən] 'the fish'; *ruskig* [ruˈskiˋg] 'disagreeable'.

Exceptions to this rule are the words *människa* [mɛˈniʂaˋ][2] 'human being', and *marskalk* [maˈʂaˋlk] 'marshal'.

---

[1] But *kanske* [kaˈnʂəˋ] 'perhaps' (= *kan ske* 'may happen').
[2] But *mänsklig* [mɛˈnskliˋg] 'human'.

31

t

The combination *ti* in words borrowed from French and Latin is pronounced:

(*a*) as [tsi] before *e* and *a*.

EXAMPLES: *aktie* [aˈktsiə] 'share'; *initiativ* [initsiatiːˈv] 'initiative'.

b) as [ṣ] (sometimes [tṣ]) in the suffix *-tion*.

EXAMPLES: *lektion* [lɛkṣωːˈn] 'lesson'; *station* [staṣωːˈn]; *nation* [natṣωːˈn].

The combination *th* (only in proper names) is pronounced as [t].

EXAMPLES: *Luther* [luˈtər]; *Thomas* [tωːˈmas].

The combination *tj* is pronounced as [ç] (see § 2 [Palatal consonants]).

EXAMPLES: *tjog* [çoːg] 'score'; *tjugo* [çɯːˈgə`] 'twenty'; *tjuv* [çɯːv] 'thief'; *tjänst* [çɛnst] 'service'.

A final *t* is mute in some words borrowed from French.

EXAMPLES: *konsert* [kɔŋsæːˈr] 'concert'; *kuvert* [kɯvæːˈr] 'envelope'; *dessert* [dɛsæːˈr] 'dessert'.

x

is pronounced as [ks] (never [gz]).

EXAMPLES: *sex* [sɛks] 'six'; *exempel* [ɛksɛˈmpəl] 'example'; *examen* [ɛksaːˈmən] 'examination'; *läxa* [lɛˈksa`] 'lesson', 'homework'.

The combination *xi* in words ending in *-xion* is pronounced as [kṣ].

EXAMPLE: *reflexion* [rɛflɛkṣωːˈn] 'reflection'.

z

is pronounced as voiceless [s]

EXAMPLES: *zoologi* [sωɔlɔgiːˈ] 'zoology'; *zink* [siŋk] 'zinc'.

Grammar

THE INDEFINITE ARTICLE 15

NON-NEUTER		NEUTER		
en son	a son	**ett** hus	a house
en gosse	a boy	**ett** äpple	an apple
en dotter	a daughter	**ett** öga	an eye
en park	a park		
en skola	a school		

The indefinite article has two forms:

en [ɛn] for non-neuter nouns;

ett [ɛt] for neuter nouns. See §§ 35—39.

THE DEFINITE ARTICLE 16

Singular

NON-NEUTER		NEUTER	
son**en**	the son	hus**et**	the house
gosse**n**	the boy	äpple**t**	the apple
park**en**	the park	öga**t**	the eye
skola**n**	the school		

The Swedish Definite Article is a **terminal article,** i. e. it is added as a termination to the Noun, and is not placed before the Noun as in English.[1]

---

[1] Cf. the definite article of the Adjective, § 78.

In the singular the Definite Article is:

-en (or **-n**) for non-neuter nouns;
-et (or **-t**) for neuter nouns.

The reduced forms (**-n** and **-t**) are used when the noun ends in a vowel, e. g. skola**n**, äpple**t** (and in a few other cases, for which see below).

Plural

INDEFINITE		DEFINITE	
(a) skolor	schools	skolor**na**	the schools
prinsar	princes	prinsar**na**	the princes
parker	parks	parker**na**	the parks
skomakare	shoemakers	skomakar**na**[1]	the shoemakers
(b) äpplen	apples	äpple**na**	the apples
(c) hus	houses	hus**en**	the houses

In the plural the Definite Article has three forms:

(a) **-na** for non-neuter nouns.

(b) **-a** for neuter nouns of the 4th Declension. See § 67.

(c) **-en** for neuter nouns of the 5th Declension. See § 70.

17 REMARKS ON THE DEFINITE SINGULAR

(1) Non-neuter nouns ending in unstressed[2] **-el, -er** take **-n** (instead of **-en**) in the definite form.

artikel	article	artikel**n**	the article
fågel	bird	fågel**n**	the bird
fjäder	feather	fjäder**n**	the feather
neger	negro	neger**n**	the negro

---

[1] The final **-e** in nouns ending in **-are** is dropped when **-na** is added.
[2] Cf. below under (4).

(2) Neuter single-tone[1] nouns ending in unstressed **-el, -er** drop the **-e** before **-l** and **-r** in the definite form.

ett segel	a sail	segl**et**	the sail
ett exempel	an example	exempl**et**	the example
ett finger	a finger	fingr**et**	the finger

NOTE. — Double-tone[1] nouns do not drop the **-e**, e. g. *papper* 'paper', *papperet* 'the paper'.

(3) Single-tone[1] nouns (non-neuters and neuters) ending in unstressed **-en** drop the **-e** when the definite article is added[2].

en botten	bottom	bottn**en**	the bottom
ett vapen	weapon	vapn**et**	the weapon
ett tecken	sign	teckn**et**	the sign

NOTE. — Double-tone nouns do not drop the **-e**, e. g. *siden* 'silk', *sidenet* 'the silk'.

(4) The following nouns take the definite article **-n** (not **-en**) although they have Tone II (and consequently weak secondary stress on the final **-el, -er**):

ängel	angel	ängel**n**	the angel
nyckel	key	nyckel**n**	the key
spegel	mirror	spegel**n**	the mirror
fader	father	fader**n**	the father
moder	mother	moder**n**	the mother
broder	brother	broder**n**	the brother
dotter	daughter	dotter**n**	the daughter
syster	sister	syster**n**	the sister

(5) The word *himmel* (Tone II) 'heaven', takes the definite form *himl***en** (sometimes *himmel***en**).

---

[1] See § 4.
[2] EXCEPTION: *examen, fröken*. See below under (12).

(*6*) In colloquial speech non-neuter nouns ending in **-are** drop the final **-e** when the terminal article **-n** is added:

skomakare**n**	(*coll.* skomakar**n**)	the shoemaker
bagare**n**	(*coll.* bagar**n**)	the baker
hammare**n**	(*coll.* hammar**n**)	the hammer

(*7*) Loan-words ending in a vowel fluctuate, e. g.:

kaféet	(*or* kafét)	the café
poesien	(*or* poesin)	poetry
filosofien	(*or* filosofin)	philosophy

(*8*) Latin nouns ending in **-or** take the definite article **-n** (not **-en**):

en doktor	doktor**n**	the doctor
en professor	professor**n**	the professor

(*9*) Latin nouns ending in **-eum, -ium** drop **-um** before the terminal article **-et**:

ett museum	muse**et**	the museum
ett laboratorium	laboratori**et**	the laboratory

(*10*) In colloquial speech some non-neuter nouns ending in **-n** or **-nd** remain unchanged in the definite form, e. g.:

botten (instead of bottn**en**)	the bottom
kapten (instead of kapten**en**)	the captain
mun (instead of mun**nen**)	the mouth
hund[1] (instead of hund**en**)	the dog
Centralstation (-station**en**)	the Central Station
Norra Station	the North Station
på julafton (-afton**en**)	on Christmas Eve

(*11*) Abstract nouns derived from Verbs and ending in **-an** take no terminal article:

början	beginning; the beginning
längtan	longing; the longing

---

[1] Colloquial pronunciation [hun]. Cf. § 11: 14.

(*12*) Some non-neuter nouns ending in **-en** take no terminal article, e. g. *examen*[1] 'examination'; *borgen* 'guarantee', 'surety'; *fröken* 'Miss'.

(*13*) In monosyllabic nouns final **-m** and **-n** preceded by a short vowel are doubled in the definite form, e. g. *kam* 'comb', *kammen* 'the comb'; *rum* 'room', *rummet* 'the room'; *man* 'man', *mannen* 'the man'; *mun* 'mouth', *munnen* 'the mouth'.

(*14*) The nouns *sjö* [ʂøː] 'lake', and *snö* [snøː] 'snow', shorten the vowel in the definite form: *sjön* [ʂœn], *snön* [snœn].

REMARKS ON THE DEFINITE PLURAL 18

(*a*) In formal style masculine nouns sometimes take the old ending **-ne** instead of **-na** in the definite plural, e. g.:

| kungar | kings | kunga**ne** (*now* kunga**na**) | the kings |
| bagare | bakers | baga**ne** (*now* baga**na**) | the bakers |

(*b*) Neuter nouns ending in unstressed **-el, -en, -er** drop the **-e** when the definite article is added in the plural, e. g.:

segel	sails	segl**en**	the sails
exempel	examples	exempl**en**	the examples
vapen	weapons	vapn**en**	the weapons
tecken	signs	teckn**en**	the signs
fönster	windows	fönstr**en**	the windows
fruntimmer	women	fruntimr**en**	the women

(*c*) Note the following **irregular plurals** (Cf. §§ 69, 73):

man	man	män	men	männen[2]	the men
gås	goose	gäss	geese	gässen	the geese
mus	mouse	möss	mice	mössen	the mice
öga	eye	ögon	eyes	ögonen	the eyes
öra	ear	öron	ears	öronen	the ears

---

[1] And other Latin nouns in **-amen**.
[2] Note that this word has double **-n-** in the definite forms, both singular and plural: *mannen* 'the man'; *männen* 'the men'.

(*d*) Note the following divergences between the written and the spoken language in the definite plural of neuter nouns (Cf. § 11: 1—2):

hus	houses	husen	(*coll.* husena)	the houses
segel	sails	seglen	(*coll.* seglena)	the sails
fönster	windows	fönstren	(*coll.* fönsterna)	the windows
ögon	eyes	ögonen	(*coll.* ögona)	the eyes
öron	ears	öronen	(*coll.* örona)	the ears

Use of the Articles

19 DEFINITE ARTICLE

In most cases the use of the definite article in Swedish corresponds to the use of the definite article in English. The following are the principal exceptions:

20 Abstract nouns used in a general sense usually take the definite article.

Konsten är lång, livet är kort.	Art is long, life is short.
Ljuset går fortare än ljudet.	Light travels faster than sound.
Tiden går.	Time flies.
Den allmänna opinionen.	Public opinion.
Han dömdes till döden.	He was sentenced to death.
Kärleken är blind.	Love is blind.
Historien upprepar sig.	History repeats itself.
Den svenska litteraturens historia.	The history of Swedish literature.

NOTE. — **Material nouns** used in a general sense often (but not always) take the definite article.

Vattnets fryspunkt.	The freezing-point of water.
Järnets egenskaper.	The properties of iron.

38

Note particularly the following nouns:

naturen	nature	himlen	heaven
försynen	Providence	helvetet	hell
ödet	fate	paradiset	paradise
kristenheten	Christendom	skärselden	purgatory
mänskligheten	humanity	människan	man (mankind)
parlamentet	Parliament	mannen	man
eftervärlden	posterity	kvinnan	woman
samhället (societeten)	society	kyrkan	church
ålderdomen	old age	skolan	school
ungdomen	youth		

EXAMPLES

Människans herravälde över naturen.	Man's mastery over Nature.
Ödet var emot honom.	Fate was against him.
Sådan är ungdomen.	Such is youth.
Fader vår, som är i himlen.	Our Father, which art in Heaven.
Människan spår, Gud rår.	Man proposes, God disposes.
Kvinnan skapades efter mannen.	Woman was created after man.
Jag går i kyrkan om söndagarna.	I go to church on Sundays.
Om vardagarna går jag i skolan.	On week-days I go to school.
Han har rest in till stan.	He has gone up to town.

NOTE. — **Plural nouns** used in a general sense take the definite article, e. g.:

Engelsmännen reser mycket.	Englishmen are great travellers.
Människorna började segla över haven.	Men began to cross the seas.
Priserna har stigit.	Prices have risen.

Names of **meals, days, seasons,** and **festivals** usually take the 22 definite article.

Jag brukar ta en promenad före frukosten.	I generally go out for a walk before breakfast.
Middagen är serverad.	Dinner is served.

39

Hon föddes fredagen den 2 maj.	She was born on Friday, May 2nd.
På lördagarna spelar vi fotboll.	On Saturdays we play football.
Våren är en härlig årstid.	Spring is a lovely season.
Om somrarna bor vi på landet.	In summer we live in the country.
Jag tillbringade julen hos mina föräldrar.	I spent Christmas with my parents.
Juldagen. Långfredagen.	Christmas Day. Good Friday.

NOTE. — Together with **äta** 'eat' names of meals do not take the definite article.

När äter ni middag?	What time do you have dinner?

23 Names of **streets, squares, parks,** and other **public places** take the definite article.[1]

Jag bor på Kungsgatan, nära Hötorget.	I live in King Street not far from the Haymarket.

Strandvägen   (a street);
Humlegården (a park in Stockholm);
Västerbron   (a bridge);

EXCEPTION: Norrbro [nɔrbrɯ:'].

24 Nouns denoting **time** and **measure** in a distributive sense take the definite article, where in English the indefinite article is used. Nouns denoting time are preceded by a preposition (*i* or *om*).

De här tavlorna kostar 500 kronor stycket (= per styck).	These pictures cost 500 kronor apiece.
Handskarna kostade sju kronor paret (= per par).	The gloves cost seven kronor a pair.
Pennorna kostar två kronor dussinet (= per dussin).	The pencils are two kronor a dozen.
Tåget går 100 kilometer i timmen.	The train travels sixty miles an hour.

---

[1] Names compounded with **-plan** ('Circus') take no definite article, e. g. *Odenplan, Karlaplan.*

Det händer endast en gång om	It only happens once a year
året (i månaden).	(a month).

Note the use of the definite form in the following expressions: **25**

Jag träffade honom förra veckan	I met him last week (month,
(månaden, året).	year).
(But: jag träffar honom nästa	(I shall be seeing him next
vecka.)	week.)
Det[1] mesta teet kommer från	Most tea comes from China.
Kina.	
De[1] flesta affärerna är stängda	Most shops are closed on
på söndagarna.	Sundays.

Nouns preceded by the epithets *båda* 'both', *vardera* 'either', and **26**
ingendera 'neither', require the definite article.

På vardera sidan (*or:* på ömse	On either side of the street.
sidor) om gatan.	
Båda pojkarna drunknade.	Both boys were drowned.

In several cases, which cannot be specially classified, an indefinite **27**
form in English corresponds to a definite form in Swedish, e. g.:

hela dagen	all day
hela natten	all night
vid soluppgången	at sunrise
om dagen	by day
om natten	by night
blind på ena ögat	blind in one eye
hälften av landet	half of the country
vara av den åsikten	to be of opinion
förlora tålamodet	lose patience
till namnet	by name
till utseendet	by sight

---

[1] See § 78.

28 The definite article in Swedish often corresponds to a possessive adjective in English, particularly in the case of nouns denoting parts of the body, clothing, etc. (things belonging to the subject in an active clause).

Hon skakade på huvud**et**.	She shook *her* head.
Jag stoppar inte kniv**en** i mun-**nen**, när jag äter.	I don't put *my* knife into *my* mouth when I eat.
Jag fryser om fötter**na**.	*My* feet are cold.
Han stoppade hand**en** i fick**an**.	He put *his* hand in *his* pocket.
Han tog av sig skor**na**.	He took off *his* shoes.

Omission of Definite Article

29 Names of **families, ships,** and **hotels** do not take the definite article.

Jag bor hos Lundströms.	I am staying at the Lundströms'.
Han reste till New York med Gripsholm.	He sailed for New York in the Gripsholm.
Han tog in på Grand.	He put up at the Grand.

NOTE. — (*a*) Names of Swedish lakes take the definite article, e. g. *Mälaren, Vänern, Vättern, Siljan.*

NOTE. — (*b*) Names of Swedish mountains and rivers fluctuate. Mountains: *Åreskutan, Kullen* (but *Omberg, Kinnekulle*). Rivers: *Dalälven, Ljusnan* (but *Lule älv*).

Note the names of two foreign rivers with the definite article: *Themsen* 'the Thames'; *Nilen* 'the Nile'. (But: *Rhen* 'the Rhine'; *Donau* 'the Danube'; *Seine; Po.*)

30 In several cases, which cannot be specially classified, a definite form in English corresponds to an indefinite form in Swedish, e. g.:

han steg av på fel (*rätt*) *station* 'he got out at the wrong (the right) station'; *jag skall stiga av vid nästa station* 'I am getting out at the next station'; *i nuvarande ögonblick* 'at the present moment'; *det är på höger* (*vänster*) *sida* 'it is on the right (left) hand side'; *håll till vänster* 'keep to the left'; *från Ystad i söder* ('in the south') *till Haparanda i norr* ('in the north'); *spela piano* 'play the piano'; *spela flöjt* 'play the flute' (but: *spela kort* 'cards'; *spela fotboll,* etc.); *ha tandvärk* 'have the toothache'; *följande dag* '/on/ the following day'; etc.

INDEFINITE ARTICLE   31

In most cases the use of the indefinite article in Swedish corresponds with the use of the indefinite article in English. Note the following exceptions (Cf. § 24):

(a) With the indefinite article: **en** *del av pengarna* 'part of the money'.

(b) Without the indefinite article: *han väntar på svar* 'he is waiting for an answer'; *han skriver brev* 'he is writing a letter'; *göra narr av någon* 'make a fool of a person'; *ha öga för* 'have an eye for'; *hurudan karl är han?* 'what sort of a man is he?'; *han hade stor lust att försöka* 'he had a great mind to try'; *jag har huvudvärk* 'I have got a headache'; *man har rätt att försvara sig* 'one has a right to defend oneself'; *göra slut på* 'put a stop to'; *vara slut* 'be at an end'; *röka pipa* 'smoke a pipe'.

(c) In Swedish the indefinite article often corresponds to English 'a piece of', e. g. *ett snöre* 'a piece of string'; *en tvål* 'a piece of soap'; *en smörgås* 'a slice of bread and butter'.

Predicative nouns denoting a person's **nationality, religion, pro-**   32
fession, trade, age etc. do not take the indefinite article. Nor is the indefinite article used after *som* in the sense of 'as', 'in the capacity of'.

Ibsen är norrman, Strindberg är svensk.	Ibsen is a Norwegian, Strindberg is a Swede.
Mannen var protestant, hans hustru katolik.	The husband was a Protestant, his wife a Roman Catholic.
Han är läkare till yrket.	He is a physician by profession.
Han blev vald **till** riksdagsman.	He was elected a Member of Parliament.
Redan **som** barn skrev han romaner.	Even as a child he wrote novels.

| Sverige börjar bli populärt **som** turistland. | Sweden is getting popular as a tourist country. |

33 The indefinite article is not used after the word *vilken* 'how' (or 'what') in **exclamations,** nor after *mången* 'many a', or *hur* 'however', + an adjective.

Vilken härlig utsikt! (*but*: En sådan härlig utsikt!)	What a splendid view!
Inser du inte, vilket oerhört misstag du har gjort?	Don't you realize what a terrible mistake you have made?
Mången gång kan det se mörkt ut.	Many a time the outlook may be dark.
Hur stort misstag jag än har gjort, /så/ har du gjort ett ännu större.	However great a mistake I have made, you have made a still greater one.

34 The indefinite article is placed **before** the adjective in expressions like the following:

en halv mil 'half a mile'; *en halv timme* 'half an hour'; *ett sådant svårt problem* 'so difficult a problem'; *vid en sådan tid* 'at such a time'; *hon var en lika skicklig politiker som Elisabet själv* 'she was as clever a politician as Elizabeth herself'; *ett alltför stort misstag* 'too great a mistake'; etc.

Gender

35 The Swedish language has four Genders: masculine, feminine, neuter, and common (= non-neuter).

The Noun is:

(*a*) **masculine,** if the pronoun **han** 'he' can be used instead of the noun, e. g. *gossen: han* 'the boy: he'.

44

(*b*) **feminine,** if the pronoun **hon** 'she' can be used instead of the noun, e. g. *flickan: hon* 'the girl: she'.

(*c*) **common,** if the pronoun **den** 'it' can be used instead of the noun, e. g. *stolen: den* 'the chair: it'.

(*d*) **neuter,** if the pronoun **det** 'it' can be used instead of the noun, e. g. *bordet: det* 'the table: it'.

In masculine, feminine, and common nouns the definite singular ends in **-n**, e. g. *gossen, flickan, stolen.*

In neuter nouns the definite singular ends in **-t**, e. g. *bordet, huset, ögat.*

Masculine are: 36

(*a*) Designations of men and male animals, e. g. *Erik; konung* 'king'; *tjur* 'bull'; *tupp* 'cock'.

(*b*) Designations of higher animals are generally treated as masculine even if they are common to males and females, e. g. *elefanten* 'the elephant'; *hästen* 'the horse'; *örnen* 'the eagle'.

Feminine are: 37

(*a*) Designations of women and female animals, e. g. *Maria; drottning* 'queen'; *ko* 'cow'; *höna* 'hen'.

(*b*) Nouns designating animals are often feminine if the nominative ends in **-a**. They may also be treated as of common gender, e. g. *råtta* 'mouse'; *duva* 'pigeon'; *fluga* 'fly'.

(*c*) A few other nouns ending in **-a,** e. g. *klocka* 'clock'; *människa* 'man' (including both man and woman).

Hur mycket är klockan? What time is it?

Hon är halv sju.   It is half past six.

Common are: 38

(*a*) Designations of things and animals (with the above exceptions) if the definite form ends in **-n,** e. g.: *fågeln* 'the bird'; *fisken*

45

'the fish'; *stolen* 'the chair'; *soffan* 'the sofa'; *morgonen* 'the morning'; *rosen* 'the rose'; *handen* 'the hand'; *foten* 'the foot'.

(b) Names of months, seasons, and festivals, e. g.: *våren* 'spring'; *sommaren* 'summer'; *hösten* 'autumn'; *vintern* 'winter'; *julen* 'Christmas'; *påsken* 'Easter'; *pingsten* 'Whitsuntide'.

(c) Names of trees, e. g.: *björken* 'the birch'; *granen* 'the spruce-tree'; *tallen* 'the Scotch fir'; *eken* 'the oak-tree'.

(d) Names of lakes, rivers, and boats, e. g.: *Mälaren* 'Lake Mälar'; *Vättern* 'Lake Vätter'; *Themsen* 'the Thames'; *Britannia; Suecia* (Cf. § 29).

(e) Nouns ending in: **-ad, -are¹, -dom, -het, -ing¹, -lek, -ion,** e. g.: *månaden* 'the month'; *hammaren* 'the hammer'; *barndomen* 'childhood'; *skönheten* 'the beauty'; *skymningen* 'dusk'; *kärleken* 'love'; *nationen* 'the nation'.

39 Neuter are:

(a) Designations of things and animals if the definite form ends in **-t,** e. g.: *fåret* 'the sheep'; *biet* 'the bee'; *lejonet* 'the lion'; *bordet* 'the table'; *fönstret* 'the window'; *taket* 'the roof'; *seglet* 'the sail'; *fingret* 'the finger'.

(b) Names of continents, countries, mountains, provinces, towns, and other inhabited places, e. g.: *Europa, Asien, England, Sverige* (Sweden), *Mont Blanc, Stockholm, London, Dalarna, Mora, Drottningholm.*

(c) The letters of the alphabet, e. g.: *ett a* 'an *a*'; *ett b* 'a *b*', etc.

(d) Nouns ending in **-eri, -on** (chiefly names of berries), **-um,** e. g.: *bryggeriet* 'the brewery'; *hallonet* 'the raspberry'; *ett helgon* 'a saint'; *ett museum* 'a museum'; *ett laboratorium* 'a laboratory'.

40 Exceptions

(a) The masculine titles ending in **-bud** and **-råd** take the **neuter** articles (def. and indef.), e. g. **ett** *sändebud* 'an ambassador'; **ett** *statsråd* 'a minister'.

---

¹ Nouns in **-are** and **-ing** denoting males are masculine: *skomakaren* 'the shoe-maker'; *ynglingen* 'the young man'. Cf. § 40 (e).

NOTE. — The **pronoun** used instead of these nouns is **han** (not *det*), e. g.:

Är statsråd**et** hemma?	Is the minister at home?
Nej, **han** har gått ut.	No, he has gone out.

(*b*) The feminine appellation *fruntimmer* 'woman' takes the **neuter** articles, but the pronoun used instead of *fruntimmer* is **hon** (not *det*), e. g.:

Det är **ett** fruntimmer[1] i tamburen.	There is a woman in the hall.
Hon ber att få tala med doktorn.	She wants to speak to the doctor.

(*c*) The noun *barn* 'child', is **neuter** (**ett** barn, barn**et**).

(*d*) Nouns like *kusin* 'cousin'; *gemål* 'consort'; *patient* 'patient', are masculine or feminine according as they refer to men or women.

(*e*) A few words ending in **-are** are neuter: **ett** altare 'an altar'; **ett** ankare 'an anchor'.

(*f*) Two nouns ending in **-on** are common: *morgon***en** 'the morning'; *afton***en** 'the evening'.

REMARKS ON GENDER   41

(*a*) Common and neuter in Swedish correspond to neuter in English.

(*b*) The pronouns **den** and **det** correspond to '**it**'.

(*c*) To know whether a noun denoting a thing or an animal is common or neuter, it is necessary to consult a dictionary. No hard and fast rules can be given.

Common are e. g.: *stol***en** 'the chair'; *boll***en** 'the ball'; *gås***en** 'the goose'; *get***en** 'the goat'.

Neuter are e. g.: *bord***et** 'the table'; *golv***et** 'the floor'; *bi***et** 'the bee'; *får***et** 'the sheep'.

---

[1] Def. form *fruntimr***et**.

42 GENITIVE

A Swedish noun has two case-forms: nominative and genitive. The nominative is also used as the objective case.

43 The **genitive** is formed by adding **-s** to the nominative. This **-s** is used with the definite and indefinite form of the noun, both singular and plural.

NOMINATIVE		GENITIVE	
en skola	a school	en skolas	of a school
skolan	the school	skolans	of the school
skolor	schools	skolors	of schools
skolorna	the schools	skolornas	of the schools

NOTE. — No apostrophe is used before this **-s.**

44 REMARKS ON THE GENITIVE

(*a*) The genitive of proper names ending in **-s** has the same form as the nominative; but in writing the genitive is indicated by an apostrophe after the final **-s,** e. g. *Johannes' evangelium* 'the Gospel according to St. John'.

(*b*) The genitive of other nouns ending in **-s,** e. g. *prins, dans,* should be avoided in the indefinite form.

(*c*) Latin names ending in **-us** often take the Latin genitive, e. g. *Pauli brev till romarna* 'St. Paul's Epistle to the Romans'; *Berzelii park* 'Berzelius' Park'; *Kristi födelse* 'the birth of Christ'.

45 USE OF THE GENITIVE

Not only nouns denoting living beings but also nouns denoting **inanimate objects** take the -s genitive. In the latter case it corresponds to the construction with 'of' in English.

Erik**s** mor. Pojken**s** far.	Eric's mother. The boy's father.
Pojkarna**s** föräldrar.	The parents of the boys.
Berge**ts** fot.	The foot of the mountain.

48

Parkens träd.	The trees of the park.
Skolans rektor.	The headmaster of the school.
Ljusets hastighet.	The rapidity of light.
Vattnets fryspunkt.	The freezing-point of water.
Årets sista dag.	The last day of the year.
Månadernas namn.	The names of the months.

NOTE. — A noun preceded by an **-s** genitive takes no terminal article. (*Bergets fot* lit. = 'the mountain's foot'.)

Even **adjectives** and **participles** used as nouns take the **-s** genitive   **46** (Cf. § 111), e. g.: *den gamles tacksamhet* 'the old man's gratitude'; *de närvarandes mening* 'the opinion of those present'.

In cases like the following the genitive is not used in Swedish.   **47**

Han bor hos ('with') sin moster.	He is staying at his aunt's.
Jag gick med receptet till närmaste apotek.	I took the prescription to the nearest chemist's.
Han gick till bageriet.	He went to the baker's.
En vän till hans far (*or:* En av hans fars vänner).	A friend of his father's.
En släkting till min hustru.	A relative of my wife's.

Cf.: *en av mina vänner* 'a friend of mine' (§ 141).

NOTE. — For use of genitive after the prepositions *till* and *i* see § 312.

EXPRESSIONS WITH 'OF': SWEDISH EQUIVALENTS

Besides expressing the possessive relationship the English preposition   **48** 'of' is used in many cases where Swedish has another preposition than *av* or no preposition at all. E. g.: *Slaget* **vid** *Trafalgar* 'the battle of Trafalgar'; *kärleken* **till** *Gud* 'the love of God'; *herr Andersson* **från** *Stockholm* 'Mr Andersson of Stockholm'; *dörren* **till** *rummet* 'the door of the room'; *gudsfruktan* 'the fear of God'; *tanken* **på** *döden* 'the thought of death'; *kunskaper* **i** *svenska* 'a knowledge of Swedish'.

Nouns denoting **quantity** are, as a rule, not followed by a preposi-   **49** tion in Swedish. E. g.:

En butelj vin 'a bottle of wine'; *en bit papper* (or *en papperslapp*) 'a piece of paper'; *en kopp te* 'a cup of tea'; *ett glas vatten* 'a glass of water'; *ett par månader* 'a couple of months'; *ett par skor* 'a pair of shoes'; *en massa pengar* 'a lot of money'; *en hel del besvär* 'a great deal of trouble'; *ett stort antal trådar* 'a great number of wires'; *en stor penningsumma* 'a large sum of money'; *ett halvt kilo smör* 'a pound of butter'; *en liter mjölk* 'two pints of milk'.

50 Note the following expressions:

Vi var fyra stycken.	There were four of us.
Giv mig två stycken.	Give me two of them.
De är för många.	There are too many of them.

51 The expressions 'a kind of', 'a sort of' are rendered by the genitives *ett slags, en sorts.*

En ny **sorts** potatis.	A new kind of potato.
Två **sorters** papper.	Two kinds of paper.
(Jag tycker inte om sådant.	I don't like that sort of thing.)
Alla möjliga **slags** människor.	All sorts and conditions of men.

52 No preposition is used between **geographical appellations,** such as *land* 'country'; *rike* 'kingdom'; *stad* 'town'; *landskap* 'province'; etc. and a following name.

Staden Göteborg.	The town of Gothenburg.
Ön Gotland ligger mitt i Öster-sjön.	The island of Gotland is situated in the middle of the Baltic.
Landskapet Dalarna.	The province of Dalarna.
Konungariket Sverige.	The kingdom of Sweden.

53 No preposition is used after the nouns *månad* 'month'; *namn* 'name'; *titel* 'title'; *rop* 'cry'; *parti* 'game', when they are followed by a name or some other qualification. Nor between an ordinal number and the name of a month.

50

En bagare vid namn Lundberg.	A baker of the name of Lundberg.
Han fick titeln professor.	The title of professor was bestowed upon him.
De spelade ett parti bridge.	They played a game of bridge.
Januari månad är den kallaste.	The month of January is the coldest.
Den tjugoförsta april.	The 21st of April.
Den sista januari.	The last of January.

No determinative pronoun is used in Swedish before a genitive in **54** cases like the following (cf. § 169):

Ljusets hastighet är större än **ljudets.**	The rapidity of light is greater than *that of sound.*

INDIRECT OBJECT

No preposition precedes the indirect object after the verbs *tillskriva* **55** 'attribute'; *meddela* 'communicate'; *synas* 'seem'; *förefalla* 'appear'; *tillhöra* 'belong'; *hända* 'happen'; *besvara* 'reply'.

Dikten har tillskrivits Tegnér.	The poem has been attributed to Tegnér.
Han meddelade mig sina iakttagelser.	He communicated his observations to me.
Oss förefaller det omöjligt.	To us it seems impossible.
Huset tillhör henne.	The house belongs to her.
Det föll honom aldrig in, att han kunde ha orätt.	It never occurred to him that he might be wrong.
Har någonting hänt pojkarna?	Has anything happened to the boys?
Han har inte besvarat (*or* svarat på) brevet.	He has not replied to the letter.

The indirect object is often used without a preposition when it is **56** governed by a predicative adjective.

51

Jag skulle bli **er** mycket förbunden.	I should be very much obliged to you.
Fienden var **oss** överlägsen i antal.	The enemy were superior to us in numbers.
De gamla visorna är **mig** lika kära som någonsin.	The old songs are as dear to me as ever.

Similarly:

Det skall bli **mig** ett nöje.	I shall be delighted.
Boken hade varit **honom** till stor nytta.	The book had been of great use to him.

57 The verb 'to tell' (= relate, narrate) is rendered by *tala om*[1] *|för|* or *säga |åt|*. When 'to tell' expresses command, it is generally translated by *säga åt* (with stress on *åt*).

Tala inte om[1] det **för** någon! Säg det inte **åt**[2] någon!	Do not tell anybody.
Vem talade om det **för** dig? Vem har sagt det?	Who told you?
Jag har någonting att **säga er**.	I have something to say to you.
Säg åt[3] honom, att han kommer hit!	Tell (= order) him to come here.
Säg åt[3] honom, att jag vill tala med honom!	Tell him that I want to speak to him.

58 The indirect object is preceded by the preposition *åt* 'to', when it comes after the direct object.

Han köpte en segelbåt **åt mig** och en ångmaskin **åt min bror**.	He bought a sailing-boat for me and a steam-engine for my brother.

NOTE. — The preposition *åt* (sometimes *till* or *för*) is also used in many cases where English has an indirect object without a preposition, e. g. *Skall jag komma upp med lite varmt vatten* **åt er**? 'Shall I bring you up some hot water?'

---

[1] The stress on *om*.

[2] Unstressed.

[3] The stress is on *åt*.

The Noun

DECLENSIONS

The Swedish language has five declensions, i. e. five different ways **59**
of forming the (indefinite) plural of nouns.

The plural of nouns belonging to the 1st Declension ends in **-or,** e. g. **60**
skola 'school' — *skol**or*** 'schools'.

The plural of nouns belonging to the 2nd Declension ends in **-ar,**
e. g. *prins* 'prince' — *prins**ar*** 'princes'.

The plural of nouns belonging to the 3rd Declension ends in **-er,**
e. g. *park* 'park' — *park**er*** 'parks'.

The plural of nouns belonging to the 4th Declension ends in **-n,**
e. g. *äpple* 'apple' — *äppl**en*** 'apples'.

The (indefinite) plural of nouns belonging to the 5th Declension
has the same form as the singular, e. g. *hus* 'house' — *hus* 'houses'.

1st DECLENSION

Plural ending: **-or** [ωr], [ər]   **61**

	SINGULAR		PLURAL	
(*a*)	en skola	a school	skolor	schools
	skolan[1]	the school	skolorna[1]	the schools
(*b*)	en ros	a rose	rosor	roses
	rosen[1]	the rose	rosorna[1]	the roses

The 1st Declension comprises: **62**

(*a*) Non-neuter nouns of more than one syllable ending in **-a,** e. g.:
*kron**a*** 'crown'; *flick**a*** 'girl'; *gat**a*** 'street'; *flagg**a*** 'flag'; *tavl**a*** 'picture'. They drop the final **-a** when the plural ending is added:
*kron**or***, *flick**or***, *gat**or***, *tavl**or***.
EXCEPTION: *histori**a*** 'story', def. form *histori**en***, plur. *histori**er***.

---
[1] The Swedish definite article is a terminal article, i. e. it is added as a termination
to the noun. See § 16.

(*b*) A few nouns ending in a consonant, e. g.:
ros 'rose'; *våg* 'wave'; *toffel* 'slipper'; *åder* 'vein'.
These have as plural: *rosor, vågor, tofflor, ådror.*

63   2nd DECLENSION

Plural ending: **-ar** [ar]

SINGULAR		PLURAL	
(*a*) en hund	a dog	hundar	dogs
hunden	the dog	hundarna	the dogs
(*b*) en ö	an island	öar	islands
ön	the island	öarna	the islands
(*c*) en gosse	a boy	gossar	boys
gossen	the boy	gossarna	the boys
en vinter	a winter	vintrar	winters
vintern	the winter	vintrarna	the winters
(*d*) en drottning	a queen	drottningar	queens
drottningen	the queen	drottningarna	the queens

64   The 2nd Declension comprises:

(*a*) Most monosyllabic non-neuter nouns ending in a consonant.

(*b*) Some monosyllabic non-neuter nouns ending in a vowel, e. g.
bro 'bridge'; *by* 'village'; *fru* 'Mrs.' or 'wife'; *sky* 'cloud'; *sjö*
'lake'; *å* 'stream'.

(*c*) Non-neuter nouns of more than one syllable ending in unstressed **-e, -el, -en** or **-er**. They drop the **-e** in the plural,
e. g. *droppe*, pl. *dropp*ar 'drop'; *fågel*, pl. *fågl*ar 'bird'; *öken*, pl.
*ökn*ar 'desert'; *seger*, pl. *segr*ar 'victory'.

(*d*) Non-neuter nouns ending in the suffixes **-dom** and **-ing,** e. g.
ungdom 'youth'; *yngling* 'young man'.

NOTE. — There is one neuter noun in this declension: *ett finger*
'a finger', pl. *fingr*ar.

(*e*) The following nouns which have **irregular plurals**:

SINGULAR		PLURAL
sommar	summer	somrar
afton	evening	aftnar
morgon	morning	morgnar
djävul	devil	djävlar
moder	mother	mödrar
dotter	daughter	döttrar

3rd DECLENSION 65

Plural ending: **-er** [ər]

	SINGULAR		PLURAL	
(*a*)	en park	a park	parker[1]	parks
	parken	the park	parkerna	the parks
(*b*)	en hand	a hand	händer[1]	hands
	handen	the hand	händerna	the hands
(*c*)	en student[2]		studenter	
	studenten		studenterna	
(*d*)	en neger	a negro	negrer	negroes
	negern	the negro	negrerna	the negroes
(*e*)	en doktor	a doctor	doktorer[3]	doctors
	doktorn	the doctor	doktorerna	the doctors
(*f*)	ett bageri	a bakery	bagerier	bakeries
	bageriet	the bakery	bagerierna	the bakeries
(*g*)	ett museum		museer	
	museet		museerna	

---

[1] Plurals of group (*a*) have Tone II. Plurals of the groups (*b*)—(*g*) have Tone I. Cf. §§ 4, 6, 7.

[2] The stress is on the last syllable.

[3] Note change of stress and tone in the plural: sing. [dɔ'ktɔˋr], plur. [dɔktω:'rər].

55

66   The 3rd Declension comprises:

(*a*) Many monosyllabic nouns ending in a consonant, e. g. *färg* 'colour'; *vers* 'verse'; *form* 'form'; *dam* 'lady'; *gräns* 'boundary'. They are pronounced with the double tone (Tone II) in the plural.

(*b*) The following nouns, which **modify their root-vowel** in the plural (Cf. Eng. *tooth — teeth*):

SINGULAR		PLURAL[1]
hand	hand	händer
and	duck	änder
brand	fire	bränder
rand	stripe	ränder
strand	beach	stränder
tand	tooth	tänder
land (n.)	country	länder
tång	pair of tongs	tänger
stång	pole	stänger
stad	town	städer
bok	book	böcker
fot	foot	fötter
rot	root	rötter
natt	night	nätter
son	son	söner (Tone II)
bokstav	letter (in the alphabet)	bokstäver (Tone II)
ledamot	member	ledamöter (Tone II)

(*c*) The following nouns, which **double the final consonant** and shorten the root-vowel in the plural:

SINGULAR		PLURAL
get [jc:t]	goat	getter (Tone I)
nöt	nut	nötter (Tone I)

---

[1] These plurals, with the exception of *söner*, *bokstäver* and *ledamöter*, are pronounced with Tone I.

56

(*d*) Non-neuter nouns formed with the suffixes **-nad, -skap,**[1] **-när, -het** and **-else,** e. g. *månad* 'month'; *kunskap* 'knowledge'; *konstnär* 'artist'; *svaghet* 'weakness'; *händelse* 'event'. The final **-e** in **-else** is dropped in the plural: *händels***er**.

(*e*) Non-neuter nouns of foreign origin (loan-words) with the stress on the last syllable, e. g. *akademi* 'academy'; *armé* 'army'; *idé* 'idea'; *metall* 'metal'; *diamant* 'diamond'; *nation* 'nation'; *patient; protestant; general.* Plur. *akademi***er**, *armé***er**, *idé***er**, etc.

(*f*) Latin nouns in **-eum** and **-ium,** e. g. *museum; laboratorium.* They drop the **-um** before the plural ending: *muse***er**; *laboratori***er**.

(*g*) Loan-words ending in **-arie** and **-ie.** These drop the **-e** before the plural ending, e. g. *bibliotekarie* 'librarian'; *aktie* 'share'. Plur. *bibliotekari***er**; *akti***er**.

(*h*) Loan-words ending in **-or,** e. g. *doktor; professor.* In the plural: *doktor***er**, *professor***er**. See footnote [2] on p. 24.

(*i*) Loan-words ending in unstressed **-el**[2], **-er,** e. g. *regel* 'rule'; *mirakel* 'miracle'; *muskel* 'muscle'; *möbel* 'piece of furniture'; *fiber* 'fibre'; *neger* 'negro'. (EXCEPTION: *tiger* 'tiger', pl. *tigrar*.) The **-e** is dropped in the plural: *regl***er**, *mirakl***er**, *muskl***er**, *möbl***er**, *fibr***er**, *negr***er**.

(*j*) Neuter nouns ending in **-eri** and **-ori,** *bryggeri* 'brewery'; *konditori* 'confectioner's shop'.

(*k*) The following nouns ending in a vowel; they form their plural by adding **-r** instead of **-er:**

SINGULAR		PLURAL
mö	maiden	mö**r**
hustru	wife	hustru**r**
jungfru	maid	jungfru**r**
ko	cow	ko**r**

---

[1] *Neuter* nouns formed with the suffix **-skap** belong to the 5th Declension (plural like singular), e. g. *ett landskap* 'a province', *många landskap* 'many provinces'.
[2] But: *spegel* (Tone II) 'mirror'; plur. *speglar.* Cf. § 64 (*c*).

SINGULAR		PLURAL
klo	claw	klor
sko	shoe	skor
tå	toe	tår
frände (Tone II)	relative	frländer (Tone I)
fiende [fiː'ɔndə`]	enemy	fiender
bonde (Tone II)	peasant	bönder (Tone I)
stadsbo	town-dweller	stadsbor

(*l*) Some nouns are used in the plural only, e. g. *grönsaker* 'vegetables'; *ränker* 'intrigues'; *ferier* 'vacation'; *finanser* 'finances'; *kalsonger* 'pants'; *specerier, viktualier* [ɑː'] 'groceries'.

67 4th DECLENSION

Plural ending: **-n**

SINGULAR		PLURAL	
(*a*) ett äpple	an apple	äpplen	apples
äpplet	the apple	äpplena	the apples
(*b*) ett bi	a bee	bin	bees
biet	the bee	bina	the bees

NOTE. — The definite article in the plural of this declension is only **-a** (instead of **-na**).

68 The 4th Declension comprises:

Neuter nouns ending in a **vowel**[1], e. g. *rike* 'kingdom'; *bälte* 'belt'; *bo* 'nest'; *spö* 'rod'; *piano; solo; konto* 'account'; *hjärta* 'heart'.

69 Two nouns in this declension have **irregular plural** forms:

SINGULAR		PLURAL	
ett öga	an eye	ögon	eyes
ögat	the eye	ögonen	the eyes
ett öra	an ear	öron	ears
örat	the ear	öronen	the ears

---

[1] Except those that end in **-eri, -ori**. See § 66 (*j*).

NOTE. — The definite article in the plural of the nouns *öga, öra* is **-en** (instead of **-a**). Cf. § 11: 1.

5th DECLENSION   70

Plural like singular

SINGULAR		PLURAL	
(*a*) ett barn	a child	barn	children
barnet	the child	barnen[1]	the children
(*b*) en bagare	a baker	bagare	bakers
bagaren	the baker	bagarna[1]	the bakers
(*c*) en resande	a traveller	resande	travellers
resanden	the traveller	resandena[1]	the travellers

The 5th Declension comprises: 71

(*a*) Neuter nouns ending in a **consonant**[2], e. g. *horn* 'horn'; *namn* 'name'; *hus* 'house'; *bad* 'bath'. Also neuter loan-words ending in a consonant, e. g. *kapital; rekord.*

(*b*) Non-neuter nouns ending in **-are** and **-ande** (mostly present participles used as nouns), e. g. *skomakare* 'shoemaker'; *resande* 'traveller'.

(*c*) Some nouns (names of peoples and professions) ending in **-er,** e. g. *belgier* 'a Belgian'; *egyptier* 'an Egyptian'; *indier* 'an Indian'; *perser* 'a Persian'; *akademiker* [e:ˈm] 'academician'; *botaniker* [ɑ:ˈ] 'botanist'; *musiker* [ɯ:ˈ] 'musician'.

(*d*) The names of the suits in cards: *klöver, ruter, hjärter, spader* 'clubs, diamonds, hearts, spades'.

(*e*) Nouns denoting measure: *en mil* 'a mile'; *en kilometer; en meter; en tum* 'an inch'; *en liter, ett ton* [tɔn], *ett pund* 'a pound'.

---

[1] See § 72. Cf. 11: 1.
[2] Except *finger* (see § 64 Note), and those in **-um** (se § 66 (*f*)).

72 The **neuter** nouns of this declension (and the word *mil*) take the definite article **-en** (instead of *-na*) in the plural: *barnen, hornen.* EXCEPTION: *huvudena* 'the heads' (sing. *huvud*). (Cf. § 11: 1—2.)

The **non-neuter** nouns ending in **-are, -ande,** and **-er** have the regular definite article **-na** in the plural: *bagarna, resandena, egyptierna.*

The final **-e** in **-are** is dropped before the definite article **-na** in the plural: *bagarna.*

73 The following nouns are **irregular** in the plural (mutation of the root vowel):

SINGULAR		PLURAL	
en man	a man	män	men
mannen[1]	the man	männen[1]	the men
en gås	a goose	gäss [jɛs]	geese
gåsen	the goose	gässen	the geese
en lus	a louse	löss	lice
lusen	the louse	lössen	the lice
en mus	a mouse	möss	mice
musen	the mouse	mössen	the mice
en fader[2]	a father	fäder[3]	fathers
fadern	the father	fäderna	the fathers
en broder[2]	a brother	bröder[3]	brothers
brodern	the brother	bröderna	the brothers

REMARKS ON NUMBER

74 The following nouns are used both in the singular and in the plural (in English only in the singular):

---

[1] Double **n** in the definite forms.
[2] Tone II.
[3] Tone I.

Han har mycket små **inkomster.**	He has a very poor income.
Kunskap är makt.	Knowledge is power.
Han har goda **kunskaper** i främmande språk.	He has a good knowledge of foreign languages.
De gjorde snabba **framsteg.**	They made rapid progress.
Är det här era **pengar?**	Is this your money?
Det var goda **nyheter!**	That is good news.
Hur går **affärerna?**	How is business?
Han gav mig många goda **råd** (många värdefulla **upplysningar**).	He gave me much good advice (a great deal of valuable information).
Möblerna består av stolar och bord.	The furniture consists of chairs and tables.

Note the **singular** form of the following nouns: 75

en sax	a pair of scissors
en tång	a pair of tongs
en passare	a pair of compasses
innehåll	contents
tack	thanks
trappa	stairs
aska	ashes
havre	oats
lön	wages, salary

Vems är den här **saxen?**	Whose are these scissors?
Flaskans **innehåll.**	The contents of the bottle.
Hjärtligt **tack** för brevet!	Many thanks for your letter.
Jag mötte honom i **trappan.**	I met him on the stairs.
Det var **mycket folk** där.	There were many people there.

The Adjective

76 INDEFINITE DECLENSION

(a) NON-NEUTER   (b) NEUTER   (c) PLURAL (both genders)

varm 'warm'   **varmt**   **varma**

(a) En varm sommar   a warm summer
(b) Ett varmt bad   a hot bath
(c) Varma somrar   warm summers

The adjective is declined according to the Indefinite Declension when the noun it qualifies is in the indefinite form (i. e. has no terminal article).

In this declension the adjective has three forms, viz.:

(a) One for the **non-neuter** singular, e. g. *varm.*
(b) One for the **neuter** singular, formed by adding **-t,** e. g. *varmt.*
(c) One for the **plural** of both genders, formed by adding **-a** to the uninflected non-neuter sing., e. g. *varma.*

The indefinite forms are also used predicatively, e. g.:

(a) Vinden är kall.   The wind is cold.
(b) Vattnet är kallt.   The water is cold.
(c) Vintrarna är kalla.   The winters are cold.

77 DEFINITE DECLENSION

Den varma sommaren   the warm summer
Det varma badet   the hot bath
De varma somrarna   the warm summers

In the Definite Declension the adjective has only one form, e. g. *varma* (the same as the plural of the Indefinite Declension).

The adjective is declined according to the Definite Declension when **78** it is used attributively before a noun in the definite form (i. e. with the terminal article). In this case the adjective is generally preceded by **the Definite Article of the Adjective,** viz.:

den for the non-neuter singular;
det for the neuter singular;
de for the plural of both genders.

It should be observed that the **Noun** takes its own (terminal) Definite **79** Article although the Adjective is preceded by **den, det, de:** *den varma sommaren, det varma badet, de varma somrarna.* The English definite article 'the' in this case corresponds to two articles in Swedish: one placed in front of the adjective, the other the usual terminal article added to the noun.

REMARKS ON THE INDEFINITE NEUTER FORM **80**
OF THE ADJECTIVE

(*a*) Adjectives that end in a stressed vowel add double **-t** in the neuter, with consequent shortening of the vowel, e. g.:

blå	blue	neuter: blått	(pl. blåa)
grå	grey	grått	(pl. gråa)
ny	new	nytt	(pl. nya)
fri	free	fritt	(pl. fria)
slö	blunt	slött	(pl. slöa)

(*b*) Adjectives that end in unstressed **-en** drop the **-n** when **-t** is added[1], e. g.:

öppen	open	neuter: öppet	(pl. öppna)
liten	small	litet	(pl. **små**)
egen	own	eget	(pl. egna)
trogen	faithful	troget	(pl. trogna)

---

[1] Cf. § 220.

(c) Adjectives that end in **-t** preceded by a consonant remain unchanged in the neuter, e. g.:

fast	firm	neuter: fast	(pl. fasta)
stolt	proud	stolt	(pl. stolta)
svart	black	svart	(pl. svarta)

(d) Monosyllabic[1] adjectives that end in **-t** preceded by a long vowel double the **-t** and shorten the vowel in the neuter, e. g.:

söt [sø:t]	sweet	neuter: sött [sœt]	(pl. söta)
våt	wet	vått	(pl. våta)
vit	white	vitt	(pl. vita)
het	hot	hett	(pl. heta)

(e) Adjectives that end in **-tt** in the uninflected form remain unchanged in the neuter, e. g.:

| trött | tired | neuter: trött | (pl. trötta) |
| lätt | easy | lätt | (pl. lätta) |

(f) Adjectives that end in **-d** preceded by a consonant drop the **-d** in the neuter[2], e. g.:

ond	evil	neuter: ont	(pl. onda)
blind	blind	blint	(pl. blinda)
hård	hard	hårt	(pl. hårda)
mild	mild	milt	(pl. milda)

(g) Adjectives that end in **-d** preceded by a long vowel substitute **-tt** for the **-d** and shorten the vowel in the neuter, e. g.:

glad	glad	neuter: glatt	(pl. glada)
röd	red	rött	(pl. röda)
bred	broad	brett	(pl. breda)
god [gω:d]	good	gott [ɔ]	(pl. goda)

(h) Adjectives that end in **-nn** drop one **-n** when **-t** is added, e. g.:

| sann | true | neuter: sant | (pl. sanna) |
| tunn | thin | tunt | (pl. tunna) |

---

[1] But dissyllabic *privat* [privɑ:'t] 'private' remains unchanged in the neuter.
[2] Cf. § 220.

(*i*) The following adjectives are not used in the neuter singular of the Indefinite Declension: *lat* 'lazy'; *rädd* 'frightened'; *höger* 'right'; *vänster* 'left'.

REMARKS ON THE FORMATION OF THE PLURAL AND THE DEFINITE FORMS OF ADJECTIVES

(*a*) Adjectives that end in unstressed **-al, -el, -en, -er** drop the vowel preceding **-l, -n, -r** when **-a** is added in the plural and in the definite form[1], e. g.:

gammal	old	plural and def. form: gamla (one **m**!)
ädel	noble	ädla
mogen	ripe	mogna
tapper	brave	tappra
vacker	beautiful	vackra

(*b*) The adjective **liten** 'little', is irregular:

Indef.	en liten flicka	a little girl
	ett litet barn	a little child
	små flickor (barn)	little girls (children)

Def.	den **lilla** flickan	the little girl
	det **lilla** barnet	the little child
	de **små** flickorna (barnen)	the little girls (children)

(*c*) With words denoting males the old masculine termination **-e** is sometimes used instead of **-a,** e. g. in the following cases:

(*1*) In exclamations and in solemn apostrophes, e. g. *Gode Gud!* 'Good God!'; *Käre vän!* 'Dear friend!'

(*2*) When the adjective is used as a noun, e. g. *den blinde* 'the blind man'; *den gamle* 'the old man'. Cf. *den blinda* 'the blind woman'; *den gamla* 'the old woman'.

(*3*) When the adjective is used after a proper name as a surname, e. g. *Karl den store* 'Charlemagne'; *Erik den helige* 'St. Eric'.

---

[1] Cf. § 220.

82 REMARKS ON THE USE OF THE INDEFINITE AND THE DEFINITE FORMS OF ADJECTIVES

The **indefinite** form of the adjective is used:

(a) after the indefinite adjectives[1]: **mången** 'many a'; **någon** 'some, any'; **ingen** 'no, not any'; **varje** 'each, every' e. g.:

mången (varje) tapper soldat	many a (every) brave soldier
ingen ovänlig handling	no unkind action
någon vänlig människa	some kind person
inget nytt instrument	no new instrument
något elakt barn	some bad child
varje stort företag	every great enterprise

(b) after **vilken** and **sådan** in exclamations, e. g.:

Vilken härlig utsikt!	What a glorious view!
Ett sådant otäckt väder!	What nasty weather!

83 The **definite** form of the adjective (but without the definite article) is used:

(a) after a **genitive**[2], e. g.:

Anderssons nya hus	Andersson's new house
hans (hennes, deras) nya hus	his (her, their) new house
husets nya (gamla) ägare	the new (old) owner of the house
Han är en man, vars goda smak man kan lita på.	He is a man whose good taste you can rely on.

(b) after a **possessive adjective**[2], e. g.:

mitt (ditt, vårt ert, sitt) lilla rum	my (thy, our, your, his) little room

(c) after **personal pronouns** in exclamations, e. g.:

Jag olyckliga människa!	I, unhappy man!
Du gamla, du fria . . .	Thou old, thou free . . . (The Swedish National Anthem.)

---

[1] See § 185.
[2] Exception: *egen* (see § 84).

(*d*) after a **demonstrative adjective**, e. g.:

detta ny**a** hus (det här ny**a**   this new house
huse**t**)

(*e*) after a **determinative adjective**, e. g.:

det ny**a** hus, som du ser där   the new house you see over
borta   there

(*f*) in **forms of address**, e. g.:

kära (*käre*) *vän!* 'dear friend!' *kära barn!* 'dear child!' *kära du*
'my dear'; *Bästa Herr Andersson!* 'Dear Mr Andersson';

(*g*) when the adjective qualifies a following **proper name**, e. g.
lilla Maria 'little Maria'; *Tjocka Berta* 'Big Bertha'.

NOTE. — In these cases the adjective has the **definite** form, but
the noun the **indefinite** form (except after the demonstrative
adjectives *den här* and *den där*, when both the adjective and the
noun take the def. form).

The adjective **egen**[1] 'own' takes the **indefinite** form after a genitive   **84**
and after a possessive adjective, e. g. *Anderssons egen bror* 'Andersson's
own brother'; *hans* (*min*, *vår*) *egen bror* 'his (my, our) own brother';
mitt (*ditt*, *vårt*, *ert*, *hans*) *eget hus* 'my (thy, our, your, his) own house';
(pl. *våra egna barn* 'our own children').

The definite article of the adjective (*den*, *det*, *de*) is sometimes omitted   **85**
(usually for the sake of brevity):

(*a*) in geographical appellations, e. g.:

Engelska kanalen   The English Channel
Förenta staterna   The United States
Atlantiska oceanen   The Atlantic Ocean
Västra Trädgårdsgatan   West Garden Street
Södra Sverige   The south of Sweden

---

[1] Cf. § 117.

(*b*) in headings, names of institutions, etc., e. g.:

Första kapitlet	Chapter I
Franska revolutionen	The French Revolution
Svenska Akademien	The Swedish Academy
Skandinaviska Banken	The Scandinavian Bank
Tekniska högskolan	The Technical College

86 The definite article of the adjective (*den, det, de*) is omitted in a number of set phrases with the adjectives *hela* 'whole'; *halva* 'half'; *dubbla* 'double'; *förra* 'last'; *sista* 'last'; *själva* '/him/self'; e. g.:

hela dagen (året, tiden)	the whole day (year, time)
halva (dubbla) summan	half (double) the sum
förra veckan (året, gången)	last week (year, time)
själva Kungen	the King himself

87 Sometimes both the definite article of the adjective and the terminal article of the noun are omitted, e. g.:

på följande sätt	in the following manner
på samma gång	at the same time
nästa vecka (år)	next week (year)
med största nöje	with the greatest pleasure
utan minsta svårighet	without the least difficulty
i närmaste stad	in the nearest town
ovannämnda adress	the above-mentioned address
nedan angivna dag	the date indicated below
närslutna skrivelse	the enclosed letter

GENITIVE OF ADJECTIVES

88 When an adjective is used as a noun, it takes the **-s** ending in the genitive, e. g.:

Han är de fattiga**s** vän.	He is a friend of the poor.
Vi tror på det goda**s** slutliga seger.	We believe in the final victory of good.

When an adjective follows after the qualified noun, the adjective **89** instead of the noun takes the genitive **-s,** e. g. *Karl den stores söner* 'the sons of Charlemagne'. Cf. §§ 111 and 121.

INDECLINABLE ADJECTIVES

Adjectives that end in **-a** and **-e** remain unchanged in the neuter **90** and in the plural, e. g.:

ringa 'humble'; *bra* 'good'; *stilla* 'quiet'; *udda* 'odd'; *äkta* 'genuine'; *samtida* 'contemporary'; *gyllene* 'golden'; *öde* 'desert'; *gängse* 'current'.

EXAMPLES: *en bra karl* 'a good fellow'; *ett bra svar* 'a good answer'; *ett samtida dokument; gängse priser* ('prices').

The adjective *stackars* does not change: *stackars flicka!* 'poor girl!'; **91** *stackars barn!* 'poor child!'; *stackars människor!* 'poor people!'.

COMPARISON OF ADJECTIVES   92

POSITIVE	COMPARATIVE	SUPERLATIVE
varm	**varmare**	**varmast**
warm	warmer	warmest
dum	**dummare**	**dummast**
stupid	more stupid	most stupid

NOTE. — English 'very' before a positive and 'much' before a comparative are both rendered in Swedish by *mycket,* e. g. *mycket varm* 'very warm'; *mycket varmare* 'much warmer'.

Most Swedish adjectives form the comparative by adding **-are** and **93** the superlative by adding **-ast** to the non-neuter (uninflected) form of the positive. These comparatives and superlatives are pronounced with Tone II. (See § 7 (*b*).) EXAMPLES:

| kall | cold | kall**are** | kall**ast** |
| stark | strong | stark**are** | stark**ast** |

ny	new	nyare	nyast
trött	tired	tröttare	tröttast
sann	true	sannare	sannast

94 If the Positive ends in unstressed **-el, -en, -er,** the **-e** before **l, n, r** is dropped in the Comparative and Superlative, e. g.:

ädel	noble	ädlare	ädlast
mogen	ripe	mognare	mognast
vacker	pretty	vackrare	vackrast

95 If the Positive ends in unstressed **-a,** this vowel is dropped in the Comparative and the Superlative. (Cf. § 97: *nära*.)

| ringa | humble | ringare | ringast |

96 The following adjectives form the comparative by adding **-re** and the superlative by adding **-st** (instead of **-are** and **-ast**). These comparatives are pronounced with Tone I. (See § 6 (*d*).)

hög	high	högre [ø:]	högst [hœkst]
grov	coarse	grövre	grövst [ø:]
stor	big	större [ə]	störst [ə]
ung	young	yngre	yngst
tung	heavy	tyngre	tyngst
lång	long	längre	längst
trång	narrow	trängre	trängst
låg	low	lägre [ε:]	lägst [ε:]
få	few	färre	—
—		smärre 'small'	—

NOTE. — These adjectives modify their root vowel in the comparative and superlative:

o is changed into **ö**
å » » » **ä**
u » » » **y**

Smärre and *färre* have double **-r** (and short **ä**).

The following adjectives have **irregular** comparison:

god (bra)	good	bätt**re**	bäst (def. form: bäst**a**)
dålig	bad	säm**re**	sämst (def. form: sämst**a**)
ond	bad, evil	vär**re**	värst (def. form: värst**a**)
gammal	old	äld**re**	äldst (def. form: äldst**a**)
liten	little, small	mind**re**	minst (def. form: minst**a**)
många pl.	many	flera (fler)	flest [ɛ] (def. form: flest**a**)
mycken	much	mera(mer)	mest [ɛ] (def. form: mest**a**)
nära	near	när**m**are	{ närmast (def. form: när- maste) näst (def. form: näst**a**) }

NOTE. — (*a*) *Mycken* is mostly used in the neuter singular form *mycket* with the meaning 'a lot of', e. g. *mycket vin* 'a lot of wine'; *mycket mat* 'a lot of food'; *mycket folk* 'a lot of people'.

NOTE. — (*b*) *Minst* corresponds to English 'smallest' and 'least'. English 'most' is rendered by *mest (den mesta, det mesta)* with singular words and *de flesta* with plural words.

Den minsta flickan.	The smallest girl.
Utan minsta svårighet.	Without the least difficulty.
Den mesta tobaken.	Most tobacco.
De flesta pojkar.	Most boys.
De flesta passagerar**na**.	Most *of the* passengers.

Some adjectives form their comparative and superlative with **mera** **98** 'more' and **mest** 'most', instead of endings, viz. adjectives that end in **-ad, -e, -isk,** and all **Participles** used as adjectives, e. g.:

POSITIVE		COMPARATIVE	SUPERLATIVE
godhjärtad	kindhearted	mera godhjärtad	mest godhjärtad
öde	desert	mera öde	mest öde
nitisk	zealous	mera nitisk	mest nitisk
älskad	beloved	mera älskad	mest älskad
tröttande	tiring	mera tröttande	mest tröttande

99 Some adjectives occur only in the comparative and the superlative, e. g.:

främre	fore-, front	främst	foremost
bakre	rear	bakerst	rearmost
inre	inner	innerst	innermost
yttre	outer	ytterst	outermost
bortre	farther	borterst	farthest
övre	upper	överst	uppermost
nedre	lower	nederst	lowest

100 English 'the... the' before comparatives is rendered by *ju... desto.*

Ju mer man har, **desto** (*or:* ju) mer vill man ha.

The more one has, the more one wants.

101 The Comparative is indeclinable. It has the same form in the neuter as in the non-neuter, the same form in the plural as in the singular, and the same form in the definite as in the indefinite declension, e. g.:

en varmare sommar	a warmer summer
ett varmare klimat	a warmer climate
varmare somrar	warmer summers
den varmare sommaren	the warmer summer
det varmare klimatet	the warmer climate
de varmare somrarna	the warmer summers

102 The indefinite form of the Superlative (ending in **-ast** or **-st**) **is indeclinable.** It can only be used predicatively (i. e. in the predicate of a sentence), e. g.:

Den här rosen är vackrast.	This rose is prettiest.
Det där trädet är högst.	That tree is tallest.
De här äpplena är mognast.	These apples are ripest.

72

The definite form of Superlatives ending in '-ast' takes the **103**
termination '-e', irrespective of gender or number, e. g.:

den varmaste sommaren   the warmest summer
det varmaste klimatet   the warmest climate
de varmaste somrarna   the warmest summers

The definite form of Superlatives ending in '-st' (instead of   **104**
'-ast') takes the termination '-a' (instead of '-e'), irrespective of
gender or number, e. g.:

den yngsta dottern   the youngest daughter
det äldsta barnet   the eldest child
de bästa eleverna   the best pupils

When used **predicatively** (i. e. in the predicate of a sentence) the   **105**
superlative may usually be declined either according to the definite
or to the indefinite declension, e. g.:

Era blommor är vackrast.   Your flowers are prettiest.
Era blommor är de vackraste.   Your flowers are the prettiest.
Det här trädet är högst.   This tree is tallest.
Det här trädet är det högsta.   This tree is the tallest.

The indefinite form must be used when the comparison refers to   **106**
different parts of the same thing, e. g.:

Här är sjön djupast.   Here the lake is deepest.

The definite form must be used when the superlative is followed by   **107**
a qualifying clause or phrase, e. g.:

De här blommorna är de vack-   These flowers are the prettiest I
raste, jag har sett.   have seen.

When used **attributively** (as an epithet) the superlative is declined   **108**
according to the **definite** declension. It is then usually preceded by
the definite article of the adjective (*den, det, de*), e. g.:

den vackraste flickan   the prettiest girl
de kallaste nätterna   the coldest nights
det största huset   the largest house

109 The definite article of the adjective (*den, det, de*) is omitted in a number of set phrases (cf. § 87), e. g.:

i främsta rummet	in the foremost place
i största hast	in great haste
i bästa fall	at best

110 REMARKS ON THE DEFINITE DECLENSION OF THE ADJECTIVE

The termination **-a** is used:

(*a*) in the definite form of **the positive**, e. g.:

den kalla vintern	the cold winter
den stora gossen	the tall boy
det lilla barnet	the little child
de röda blommorna	the red flowers

(*b*) in the definite form of **the superlatives that end in '-st'**, e. g.:

det högsta berget	the highest mountain
den största gossen	the tallest boy
de minsta rummen	the smallest rooms

The termination **-e** is used:

(*a*) in the definite form of **the superlatives that end in '-ast'**, e. g.:

den starkaste gossen	the strongest boy
den vackraste flickan	the prettiest girl
det mörkaste molnet	the darkest cloud
de rikaste personerna	the richest people

(*b*) sometimes in the definite form of the positive and the superlative in **-st** when qualifying words denoting males, especially in elevated style (see § 81 *c*), e. g.:

den ädle lorden	the noble lord
den store mannen	the great man
den Högste	The Most High

74

den yngste brodern	the youngest brother
den gamle	the old man
(Cf. den gamla	the old woman)
den rike	the rich man
(Cf. de rika	the rich)
Karl den store	Charlemagne
Erik den helige	St. Eric

GENITIVE OF ADJECTIVES. Cf. § 121.

The Adjective takes an **-s** in the genitive in the following cases: **111**

(a) When it follows the noun it qualifies, e. g.:

| Erik den heliges död. | The death of St. Eric. |

(b) When it is used as a noun, e. g.:

| De fattigas vän. | The friend of the poor. |
| Den starkastes rätt. | The right of the strongest. |

RELICS OF OLD CASE-ENDINGS

Relics of the old case-inflection of the adjective have been preserved **112**
in a few set phrases, e. g.:

(a) the dative termination **-om** in:

I sinom tid.	In due season.
Lyckan står dem djärvom bi.	Fortune favours the brave.
Det är icke allom givet.	It is not everybody's lot.

(b) the accusative termination **-an** in:

| I ljusan låga. | All ablaze. |
| Argan [a'rja'n] list. | Wicked cunning. |

(c) the dative termination **-o** in:

Fräls oss ifrån ondo!	Deliver us from evil.
I godo.	Amicably.
Ånyo.	Afresh.

ADJECTIVES USED AS NOUNS

113 In English only a few adjectives used as nouns take the plural termination **-s,** e. g. 'the blacks and the whites'. In Swedish all adjectives used as nouns take the termination **-a** (sometimes **-e**) in the plural, e. g. *de fattig*a 'the poor'; *de rik*a 'the rich'.

114 Many English adjectives used as nouns, particularly those denoting **nationality,** are in Swedish expressed by **nouns,** e. g.:

infödingarna (en inföding)	the natives
vildarna (en vilde)	the savages
kineserna (en kines)	the Chinese
italienarna (en italienare)	the Italians
engelsmännen[1] (en engelsman)	the English
norrmännen (en norrman)	the Norwegians
fransmännen (en fransman)	the French
tyskarna (en tysk)	the Germans
ryssarna (en ryss)	the Russians

The corresponding adjectives in Swedish are: *kinesisk, italiensk, engelsk, norsk, fransk, tysk, rysk.*

NOTE. — (*a*) These adjectives and nouns are not written with capital letters in Swedish.

NOTE. — (*b*) The word *svensk* 'Swedish, Swede', is both adjective and noun. As a noun it is inflected according to the 2nd Declension: *en svensk, svensk***en,** *svensk***ar,** *svensk***arna.** When used adjectivally it is inflected like an ordinary adjective.

115 Most Swedish adjectives may be used as nouns without the restrictions observed in English.

Att förena det nyttiga med det nöjsamma.	To combine the useful with the agreeable.
De rika och de fattiga.	The rich and the poor.
En blind och en dövstum bodde tillsammans.	A blind man and a deaf-and-dumb man lived together.

---

[1] Never *de engelska!*

76

Vi **unga** kan inte förstå de gamla.	We young people cannot understand old people.
Det var **det enda,** han kunde göra.	It was the only thing he could do.
Han var **den enda** närvarande.	He was the only person present.
Han insåg **det fördelaktiga** i erbjudandet.	He saw the advantage of the offer.
Det nya i boken är icke sant, och **det sanna** är icke nytt.	What is new in the book is not true, and what is true is not new.
De närvarande undertecknade en petition.	Those present signed a petition.
Det är det, som är **det svåraste.**	That is what is most difficult.
Den okände kom icke tillbaka.	The unknown man did not come back.

The word *one* which often replaces a noun after an adjective in **116** English, has no equivalent in Swedish.

Den där bollen är inte bra; du skall få en ny.	That ball is not good; you shall have a new one.
Han var den enda, som kunde göra det.	He was the only one who could do it.
Ge mig en vit kula och två svarta.	Give me one white marble and two black ones.
Vi måste ta hand om de små.	We must take care of the little ones.
Den Onde.	The Evil One.

The adjective *egen* 'own', is used in the indefinite form after a genitive **117** or a possessive adjective (see § 84). Note the use of *egen* not preceded by a genitive or a possessive adjective.

Han har egen bil.	He has got a car of his own.
De bor i eget hus.	They live in a house of their own.
Han har två egna barn.	He has got two children of his own.

118 In Swedish the comparative is often used in an absolute sense ('**Absolute Comparative**') expressing no real comparison, but corresponding to *rather + positive* in English, e. g.: *en större penningsumma* 'a largish sum of money'; *en yngre herre* 'a youngish gentleman'; *bättre folk* 'gentlepeople'; *en längre tid* 'a goodish while'.

INFLECTION OF PARTICIPLES

I. — The Past Participle (see § 220)

119 *Indefinite Declension*

(*a*) Past Participles ending in **-ad** (1st Conjugation).
The neuter singular is formed by changing the final **-d** into **-t,** and the plural is formed by adding **-e** (not **-a**!) to the non-neuter singular, e. g.:

Blandad frukt.	Mixed fruit.
Ett blandat tåg.	A mixed train.
Blandade känslor.	Mingled feelings.

(*b*) Past Participles ending in **-d** (2nd Conjugation).
The neuter singular is formed by changing the final **-d** into **-t,** and the plural is formed by adding **-a** to the non-neuter singular, e. g.:

En höjd lön.	A raised salary.
Ett höjt arvode.	An increased remuneration.
Höjda löner.	Raised salaries.

(*c*) Past Participles ending in **-t** (2nd Conjugation).
The neuter singular remains unchanged, while the plural is formed by adding **-a,** e. g.:

En märkt näsduk.	A marked handkerchief.
Ett märkt lakan.	A marked sheet.
Märkta näsdukar.	Marked handkerchiefs.

(*d*) Past Participles ending in **-dd** (3rd Conjugation).
The neuter singular is formed by changing the final **-dd** into
-tt, and the plural is formed by adding **-a** to the non-neuter
singular, e. g.:

En bebodd [bəbɯ'd] ö.	An inhabited island.
Ett bebo**tt** område.	An inhabited area.
Bebodd**a** öar.	Inhabited islands.

(*e*) Past Participles ending in **-en** (4th Conjugation).
The neuter singular is formed by changing the final **-n** into **-t,**
and the plural is formed by adding **-a** to the non-neuter singular.[1]

En stulen klocka.	A stolen watch.
Ett stule**t** paraply.	A stolen umbrella.
Stuln**a** klockor.	Stolen watches.

NOTE. — In the plural the termination **-a** is used for all the
Past Participles except those ending in **-ad** (1st Conjugation),
e. g.: *höjda, märkta, bebodda, stulna*; but *blandade, kallade.*

Definite Declension   120

The definite forms of Past Participles are like the plural forms of the
indefinite declension, viz.:

(*a*) Past Participles ending in **-ad** (1st Conjugation) add **-e** in the
definite declension, e. g.:

Den blandad**e** frukten.	The mixed fruit.
Det jagad**e** lejonet.	The hunted lion.
De förlorad**e** pengarna.	The lost money.

(*b*) All other Past Participles add **-a** in the definite declension, e. g.:
Den höjd**a** lön**en**. Det höjd**a** arvode**t**. De höjd**a** löner**na**. Den
märkt**a** näsduk**en**. Det märkt**a** lakane**t**. De märkt**a** näsdukar**na**.
Den bebodd**a** ö**n**. Det bebodd**a** område**t**. De bebodd**a** öar**na**.
Den stuln**a** klocka**n**. Det stuln**a** paraply**et**. De stuln**a** klockor**na**.

---

[1] Cf. §§ 80 (*b*) and 81 (*a*).

All Past Participles used as nouns, take **-s** in the genitive, e. g.:

Den älskades namn.	The name of the beloved one.
Det stulnas värde.	The value of the stolen property.

II. — The Present Participle (see § 221)

122 The Present Participle, when used as an adjective, is indeclinable, e. g.:

Den uppgående solen.	The rising sun.
Det leende ansiktet.	The smiling face.
Ett rytande lejon.	A roaring lion.
De badande barnen.	The bathing children.

When used as a noun, the Present Participle is declined according to the 5th Declension (see §§ 70—71) and takes **-s** in the genitive, e. g.:

De närvarandes namn antecknades.	The names of those present were taken down.

Numerals

123

CARDINAL NUMBERS	ORDINAL NUMBERS
0. noll [nɔl]	
1. en [ɛn], *neuter* ett [ɛt]	(den, det) första [fə'ʂtaˋ]
2. två [tvoː]	andra [a'ndraˋ]
3. tre [treː]	tredje [treː'djəˋ]
4. fyra [fyː'raˋ]	fjärde [fjæː'ɖəˋ]
5. fem [fɛm]	femte
6. sex [sɛks]	sjätte [ʂɛ'təˋ]
7. sju [ʂɯː]	sjunde [ʂu'ndəˋ]
8. åtta [ɔ'taˋ]	åttonde [ɔ'tɔndəˋ]
9. nio [niː'əˋ]	nionde [niː'ɔndəˋ]
10. tio [tiː'əˋ]	tionde

11. elva [ɛ'lva`]	elfte
12. tolv [tɔlv]	tolfte
13. tretton [trɛ'tɔ`n]	trettonde
14. fjorton [fjω:'tɔ`n]	fjortonde
15. femton [fɛ'mtɔ`n]	femtonde
16. sexton [sɛ'kstɔ`n]	sextonde
17. sjutton [ʂu'tɔ`n]	sjuttonde [ʂu'tɔndə`]
18. aderton [ɑ:'tɔ`n]	adertonde
19. nitton [ni'tɔ`n]	nittonde
20. tjugo [çɯ:'gə`]	tjugonde [çɯ:'gɔndə`]
21. tjugoen (-ett) [çɯgəɛ'n]	tjugoförsta [çɯgəfə'ʂta`]
22. tjugotvå [çɯgətvo:']	tjugoandra
23. tjugotre	tjugotredje
24. tjugofyra	tjugofjärde
25. tjugofem	tjugofemte
26. tjugosex	tjugosjätte
27. tjugosju	tjugosjunde
28. tjugoåtta	tjugoåttonde
29. tjugonio	tjugonionde
30. trettio [trɛ'ti`]	trettionde [trɛ'tiɔ`ndə]
31. trettioen, etc. [trɛtiɛ'n]	trettioförsta, etc. [trɛti- fə'ʂta`]
40. fyrtio [fə'ʈi`]	fyrtionde
50. femtio [fɛ'mti`]	femtionde
60. sextio	sextionde
70. sjuttio	sjuttionde
80. åttio	åttionde
90. nittio	nittionde
100. (ett) hundra [hu'ndra]	(ett) hundrade [hu'ndradə]
101. (ett) hundraen (-ett)	(ett) hundraförsta
1 000. (ett) tusen [tɯ:'sən]	(ett) tusende [tɯ:'səndə]
1 001. (ett) tusenen (-ett)	(ett) tusenförsta
1 002. (ett) tusentvå, etc.	(ett) tusenandra, etc.
1 675. ettusensexhundra- sjuttiofem	etttusensexhundra- sjuttiofemte
1 000 000. en miljon [miljω:'n]	miljonte [miljω:'ntə]

NOTE. — (*a*) *Den första* and *den andra* sometimes end in -e in the masculine: *Karl I* (*den förste*), *Karl II* (*den andre*).

NOTE. — (*b*) *Ett hundra* and *ett tusen* are really nouns. They remain unchanged in the plural: *tre hundra, fyra tusen.*

NOTE. — (*c*) *En miljon* is a noun of the 3rd Declension. Plural: *två miljoner,* etc.

NOTE. — (*d*) *En gång* 'once'; *två gånger* 'twice'; *tre gånger* 'three times'.

124 THE NUMERALS IN DATES. TIME BY THE CLOCK

Jag **är** född den 13 (trettonde) maj 1947 (nittonhundrafyrtiosju).	I was born on May 13th, 1947.
År[1] 1066 (tiohundrasextiosex) erövrades England.	In[2] 1066 England was conquered.
Stockholm den 19 (nittonde) april[2] 1962 (nittonhundrasextiotvå).	Stockholm, 19th April, 1962.
Han anlände den tredje augusti.	He arrived on[2] Aug. 3rd.

NOTE. — Names of months are spelt with small letters.

Hur mycket är klockan? Vad är klockan?	What time is it?
Klockan är (**Hon** är) tre.	It is three o'clock.
Klockan är **halv fyra.**	It is half past three.
Han reste halv ett.	He left at[2] half past twelve.
Fem /minuter/ över två.	Five /minutes/ past two.
Tio /minuter/ i två.	Ten /minutes/ to two.
En kvart över elva.	A quarter past eleven.
En kvart i tolv.	A quarter to twelve.
Fem i halv sju.	Twenty-five past six.
En kvart.	A quarter of an hour.
En halvtimme.	Half an hour.
En och en halv timme.	An hour and a half.

---

[1] The word *är* may be omitted.
[2] No preposition in Swedish.

82

THE NUMERALS AS NOUNS. DOZEN. SCORE

Jag kan inte skilja dina ett**or** från dina sju**or**.	I cannot tell your ones from your sevens.

When used as nouns the numerals 1—10 add an **-a** and are treated as nouns of the 1st Declension: *en etta* [ɛ'ta`], *tvåa, trea, fyra, femma, sexa, sjua, åtta, nia, tia.* The figure *0* as a noun is called *en nolla.* Definite form: *ettan, nollan,* etc. Plural: *ettorna, tvåorna,* etc.

Åttiotalet var realismens period.	The eighties were the period of realism.
Han levde på **1700-talet** (sjutton-hundratalet).	He lived in the **18th** century.
Hundratals människor blev dödade.	Hundreds of[1] people were killed.
Fabrikerna sysselsätter **tusentals** arbetare.	The factories employ thousands of[1] workers.
De tios råd.	The council of ten.
Det är inte ens fel, att två träter.	It takes two to make a quarrel.
Den ena är sju år, den andra är nio.	One is seven years old, the other is nine.
Ett dussin. Två dussin knivar.	A dozen. Two dozen knives.
Ett tjog. Tre tjog ägg.	A score. Three score of[1] eggs.
Dussin**tals** knivar.	Dozens of knives.
Tjog**tals** ägg.	Scores of eggs.

FRACTIONS

126

$\frac{1}{2}$ *en halv*; $\frac{2}{2}$ *två halva*; $\frac{1}{3}$ *en tredjedel*; $\frac{2}{3}$ *två tredjedelar*; $\frac{5}{6}$ *fem sjättedelar*; $\frac{4}{8}$ *fyra åttondelar*; $\frac{3}{9}$ *tre niondelar*; $\frac{3}{21}$ *tre tjugoendelar.*

Most of the fractions are formed by adding **-del** 'part', to the ordinal numbers. If the ordinal number ends in **-de,** the **-de** is dropped before **-del** (except in *fjärdedel* and *sjundedel*).

---

[1] No preposition in Swedish.

Note the following expressions:

Fem och en halv mil.	Five miles and a half.
Tre och ett halvt ton.	Three tons and a half.
Två och ett kvarts [kvaṭṣ] kilo kaffe.	Two kilos and a quarter of coffee.
En och en tredjedels mil.	A mile and a third.
En hälft.	A half.
Hälften av arbetet.	Half the work.

Pronouns

127 PERSONAL PRONOUNS

SINGULAR

1ST PERSON			2ND PERSON	
SUBJ. **jag** [jɑː/g/]	I		**du** [dɯː]; **ni** [niː]	thou; you
GEN. — —[1]			— —[1]	
OBJ. **mig** [miːg, mɛj]	me		**dig** [diːg, dɛj]; **er**[2] [eːr]	thee; you

3RD PERSON				
SUBJ. **han** [han]	he		**hon** [hɯn]	she
GEN. **hans**	his		**hennes** [hɛˈnəˋs]	her
OBJ. **honom** [hɔˈnɔˋm]	him		**henne**	her
den [dɛn]	it		**det** [deː/t/]	it
dess	its		**dess**	its
den	it		**det**	it

---

[1] Instead of the missing genitives of the first and second persons the possessive adjectives (**min**; **din**; **er**) are used (see § 138).
[2] The full form **eder** [eːˈdər] is only used in formal style.

SUBJ.	**vi**	we	**ni**	you	**de** [de:, dɔm, di:]	they
GEN.	—	—[1]	—	—[1]	**deras** [de:'ra`s]	their
OBJ.	**oss**	us	**er**	you	**dem** [dɛm, dɔm]	them

NOTE. — (*a*) The object forms (**mig, dig, honom,** etc.) are used as objects and after prepositions.

NOTE. — (*b*) The genitives *hans, hennes, dess, deras* are indeclinable.

Du is used between intimate friends and members of the family   **128** (like French *tu* and German *du*). The use of *du*, however, is spreading among young people of the same class (students, workmen, etc.)

Ni (in the singular) is not generally accepted as a form of address   **129** like 'you' in English. It is always correct when speaking to a stranger or to one's inferiors. If you know the title, profession or name of the individual addressed, it is considered more polite to use the title (in the definite form) or name, as if speaking *of* the person instead of *to* him.

Talar ni svenska?	Do you speak Swedish?
Ni kan inte komma dit i kväll.	You cannot get there tonight.
Har professor**n** varit i London?	Have you been in London?
Har generalkonsul**n** sett tidningen för idag?	Have you seen today's paper?
Har grev**en** (*the Count*) varit på teatern nyligen?	Have you been to the theatre lately?
Vill fru Andersson dricka en kopp te?	Would you like a cup of tea, Mrs. Andersson?
Har herr Pettersson en tändsticka?	Have you got a match, Mr. Pettersson?

---

[1] Instead of the missing genitives of the first and second persons the possessive adjectives (**vår; er**) are used.

130 The pronoun **I** instead of *ni* in the plural is used in elevated style (in the Bible, in poetry, etc.). It is followed by a special form of the verb ending in **-en** : *I ären, I haden,* etc. 'Ye are, Ye had'.

131 In formal correspondence *Ni* and *E/de/r* are written with capitals.

132 **'Den' refers to a noun of the common (non-neuter) gender**

Var är boken? **Den** ligger på bordet.

Where is the book? — It is on the table.

'Det' refers to a noun of neuter gender

Var ligger hotell**et**? **Det** ligger vid Strandvägen.

Where is the hotel? It's in the Strand/way/.

133 In colloquial speech the enclitic (affixed) forms **'en, 'n** are sometimes used instead of *honom, den;* **'et, 't** instead of *det.*

Ja/g/ såg**'en** (såg honom) inte.
I did not see him (*or* it).

Ja/g/ la**'n** (lade den) där.
I put it there.

Vill du ha**'t** (ha det), så ta**'t**.
If you want it, take it.

Har du funderat på**'t**?
Have you thought it over?

134 **The Use of 'det'**

(*a*) **Det** = 'it'; when stressed = 'that'.

Vad är **det**? — **Det** är ett flygplan.
What is that? — It is an aeroplane.

Hurdant väder är **det** i dag? — **Det** snöar (regnar).
What sort of weather is it today? — It is snowing (raining).

Det blåser mycket.
It is very windy.

Det är sju mil till Uppsala.
It is seven Swedish miles to Uppsala.

Det är många år, sedan jag såg honom.	It is many years since I saw him.
Det är svårt att tala svenska.	It is difficult to speak Swedish.
Det var min syster, som gjorde det.	It was my sister who did it.
Det var *det* jag ville veta.	That's what I wanted to know.

(b) **Det** = 'there' (provisional subject: *det är, det finns* = 'there is', 'there are').

Det är en klocka i hallen.	There is a clock in the hall.
Det är[1] två klockor i hallen.	There are two clocks in the hall.
Det var en gång en gosse.	Once upon a time there was a boy.
Det finns ingenting kvar.	There is nothing left.
Det finns[1] 500 böcker i biblioteket.	There are 500 books in the library.
Det var[1] tre ringar i asken.	There were three rings in the box.
Det fanns inget postkontor i den byn.	There was no post-office in that village.
Är **det** något fel med det?	Is there anything the matter with it?

(c) **Det** = 'he', 'she' *or* 'they'.

Vem är Mr Smith? — **Det** är en professor i engelska.	Who is Mr Smith? — He is a professor of English.
Vem är den där damen? — **Det** är en släkting till mig.	Who is that lady? — She is a relative of mine.
Vilka är de där herrarna? — **Det är** svenskar.	Who are those gentlemen? — They are Swedes.

(d) **Det** = 'so'.

Jag är sömnig. — **Det** är jag också.	I am sleepy. — So am I.
Han har egen bil, och **det** har vi också.	He has got a car of his own, and so have we.

---

[1] After *det* the verb takes the singular form.

Är doktorn inne? — Ja, jag tror **det**.	Is the doctor in? — Yes, I think so.
Jag sa' honom **det**.	I told him so.
Sa' han **det**?	Did he say so?
Jag hoppas (tror, förmodar) **det**.	I hope (believe, suppose) so.

(e) **Det** without an equivalent in English.

In questions and answers *det* is used as predicate complement of *vara* 'be' and as object of the Auxiliary Verbs and *göra* 'do' (replacing another verb); often also as object of the verbs *fråga* 'ask', *veta* 'know' and *tala om* 'tell'.

Är du sjuk? — Ja, **det** är jag.	Are you ill? — Yes, I am.
Han har ju rest till Frankrike, eller hur? — Ja, **det** har han.	He has gone to France, hasn't he? — Yes, he has.
Han tycker om att resa, men **det** gör inte jag.	He is fond of travelling, but I am not.
Var snäll och hälsa era föräldrar. — Tack, **det** skall jag göra.	Please remember me to your parents. — I will, thank you.
Måste jag göra det nu? — Ja, **det** måste du.	Must I do it now? — Yes, you must.
Kunde han komma? — Nej, **det** kunde han inte.	Could he come? — No, he couldn't.
Han frågade henne, om hon var ond, och hon sade, att hon var **det**.	He asked her if she was angry, and she said she was.
Hur mycket är klockan? — **Det** vet jag inte.	What time is it? — I don't know.
Varför frågar du **det**?	Why do you ask?
Vem talade om **det** för dig?	Who told you?

135 Impersonal Construction

Phrases like 'I am glad', 'I am sorry', etc., are often rendered by an impersonal construction with **det** in Swedish.

Det var[1] **tråkigt,** att du inte kan komma.	I am sorry you cannot come.
Det var[1] **roligt,** att han är bättre.	I am glad he is better.
Hur står det till?	How are you?
Det ska bli roligt att få träffa honom.	I am looking forward to seeing him.
Det är bäst, att du frågar henne.	You had better ask her.
Hur går det för er?	How are you getting on?
Det gick mycket bra för honom.	He did very well.
Det förvånar mig, att han inte gjorde det.	I am surprised he didn't do it.
Det var kallt i vattnet.	The water was cold.[2]
Det knackar på dörren.	There is a knock at the door.

REFLEXIVE PRONOUNS

There are in Swedish no special reflexive pronouns for the first and **136** second persons (singular and plural). The ordinary objective forms of the personal pronouns (*mig, dig, er, oss*) are used also in a reflexive sense, corresponding to the English 'myself, yourself, yourselves, ourselves'.

Jag försvarar **mig.**	I defend myself.
Du försvarar **dig.**	You defend yourself.
Ni (singular) försvarar **er.**	You defend yourself.
Ni (plural) försvarar **er.**	You defend yourselves.
Vi försvarar **oss.**	We defend ourselves.

For the third person (singular and plural) there is a special reflexive **137** pronoun, viz. **sig** [siːg, sɛj], which must be used to refer back to the subject of the clause in which it occurs (as an object or in a prepositional phrase). It usually corresponds to the English 'himself, herself, itself, themselves'.

---

[1] Note the past tense. See § 245.
[2] When bathing in the sea.

Han försvarar **sig**.	He defends himself.
Hon försvarar **sig**.	She defends herself.
Barnet försvarar **sig**.	The child defends itself.
Hunden försvarar **sig**.	The dog defends itself.
Pojkarna försvarar **sig**.	The boys defend themselves.
Man måste försvara **sig**.	One must defend oneself.
Det är nödvändigt att kunna försvara **sig**.	It is necessary to be able to defend oneself.
Han såg en dam framför **sig**.	He saw a lady in front of him.
Hon såg **sig** omkring.	She looked about her.
De tog med **sig** en lykta.	They took a lantern with them.

NOTE. — If the object is another person than the subject, the ordinary objective forms of the personal pronouns (*honom, henne, den, det, dem*) must be used, e. g. *han försvarade honom* 'he defended him'; *hon försvarade henne* 'she defended her'; *de försvarade dem* 'they defended them'.

138 **POSSESSIVE ADJECTIVES** (Cf. §§ 28, 143—145)

SINGULAR		PLURAL
NON-NEUTER	NEUTER	BOTH GENDERS
min [min]	**mitt**	**mina** [mi:'na`] my
din [din]	**ditt**	**dina** [di:'na`] thy, your
vår	**vårt**	**våra** our
{er [e:r]	**ert** [e:ţ]	**era** [e:'ra`] your
{Eder [e:'dər]	**Edert**	**Edra** [e:'dra`] your

Det där är **min** (din) bok.	That is my (your) book.
Det här är **mitt** (ditt) glas.	This is my (your) glass.
Det här är **mina** (våra) böcker.	These are my (our) books.
Är det där **er** hatt?	Is that your hat?
Är det där **era** väskor?	Are those your bags?
Vår kung. **Vårt** land.	Our King. Our country.
Våra vänner.	Our friends.

90

REMARKS ON THE POSSESSIVE ADJECTIVES

(a) **Er** (**ert, era**) refers to one or several possessors and corresponds to the personal pronoun **ni.**

(b) The longer form **Eder** (**Edert, Edra**) is only used in formal style. An old form *E/de/rs* occurs in *E/de/rs Majestät* 'Your Majesty'.

(c) Instead of the missing Possessive Adjectives for the third person, the genitives of the Personal Pronouns of the third person are used: **hans, hennes, dess, deras.** These are indeclinable. (Cf. §§ 143—145.)

(d) The Possessive Adjectives are declined like ordinary adjectives, but are only used in the indefinite declension. In the plural they may be used as Nouns and are then preceded by the Definite Article of the Adjective, e. g. *jag och* **de mina** 'I and my people'; **de dina** 'your people', etc.

There are no special forms for the possessive adjectives when used **139** without nouns, such as the English 'mine', 'yours', etc.

Den där boken är **min** (din).	That book is mine (yours).
Din tillgivne ...	Yours sincerely ...
(Högaktningsfullt ...	Yours faithfully ...)
Ert hus är större än **mitt.**	Your house is larger than mine.
Det är inte **vårt**; det är deras.	It is not ours; it is theirs.
Våra rosor är bättre än hennes.	Our roses are better than hers.
Era rosor är bättre än **våra.**	Your roses are better than ours.
Hans bil är större än **vår.**	His car is larger than ours.

Notice the peculiar use of the Possessive Adjectives in expressions **140** like the following: *din idiot* 'you idiot'; *din dumma åsna* 'silly ass'; *jag, min dumsnut, trodde vad han sade* 'fool that I was, I believed what he said'.

The English construction 'a friend of mine' is not used in Swedish. **141** It must be expressed in other ways.

Han är en god **vän till mig.**	He is a friend of mine.
En av era elever.	A pupil of yours.
Några av mina vänner.	Some friends of mine.
Vem är den där unge mannen?	Who is that young man? — He
— Det är en släkting till oss.	is a relation of ours.
En gammal bekant till dig (er).	An old acquaintance of yours.

142 Note the following expressions:

Jag kunde inte för mitt liv begripa, vad han menade.	For the life of me I could not understand what he meant.
Det kommer att bli min död.	It will be the death of me.
Dina gelikar.	The likes of you.

143 POSSESSIVE REFLEXIVE ADJECTIVE

NON-NEUTER	NEUTER	PLURAL	
sin [sin]	**sitt**	**sina** [si:'na`]	his, her, its, their

144 **Sin** (*sitt, sina*) corresponds to the reflexive personal pronoun **sig.** It refers back to the subject of the clause in which it occurs (not to the subject of a previous clause). The subject may be one or several possessors in the third person.

Sin (*sitt, sina*) can only be used to qualify the object of a verb or preposition (never the subject!)

145 When English 'his', 'her', 'its', 'their' are not used reflexively, i. e. when they do not refer back to the subject of the clause in which they occur, they are rendered by the genitives of the personal pronouns: **hans, hennes, dess, deras.** Only these genitives can be used to qualify the *subject* of a clause.

92

Han såg **sin** far på gatan.	He saw his (own) father in the street.
Hans[1] far gick ut.	His father went out.
Han såg **hans** far på gatan.	He saw his (another person's) father in the street.
Han såg **sin** far gå ut.	He saw his (own) father go out.
Han såg, att **hans**[1] far gick ut.	He saw that his (own or somebody else's) father went out.
Hon såg **sin** far gå ut.	She saw her (own) father go out.
Hon såg, att **hennes**[1] far gick ut.	She saw that her (own or somebody else's) father went out.
Hennes[2] barn var där.	Her children were there.
Hennes[1] bok låg på bordet.	Her book lay on the table.
Hon lade **sin** bok på bordet.	She put her (own) book on the table.
Hon lade **hennes** bok på bordet.	She put her (another person's) book on the table.
Deras[2] föräldrar är i Amerika.	Their parents are in America.
De har inte sett **sina** föräldrar på flera år.	They have not seen their (own) parents for several years.
Jag har aldrig sett **deras** föräldrar.	I have never seen their parents.
De har förlorat **sitt** enda barn.	They have lost their only child.
Han bor hos en av **sina** vänner.	He is staying with a friend of his.
Hon stod och talade med **sin** mor.	She was talking to her mother.

REMARKS ON THE PERSONAL PRONOUNS AND
THE POSSESSIVE ADJECTIVES

The English form 'her' corresponds to **hennes, henne** and **sin** in **146**
Swedish.

---

[1] Not *sin!*
[2] Not *sina!*

Hennes mor är död.	Her mother is dead.
Jag har aldrig sett **henne.**	I have never seen her.
Hon har förlorat **sin** mor.	She has lost her mother.

147 The Swedish form **er** corresponds to 'you', 'your' and 'yours' in English.

Det var roligt att träffa **er.**	I am glad to meet you.
Ni har glömt **er** hatt.	You have forgotten your hat.
Jag har tagit **er,** och han har tagit min.	I have taken yours, and he has taken mine.

148 A pleonastic (redundant) *mig* occurs in expressions like the following:

Det var **mig** en dum en!	What a fool!

149 A Personal Pronoun may be qualified by an adjective.

Tack, **kära du!**	Thank you, my dear!
Stackars dig (du)!	Poor you!

150 In cases like the following, where the ownership is implied in the context, the definite article of the noun corresponds to a possessive adjective in English. (Cf. § 28.)

Han stoppade händer**na** i fickor**na.**	He put his hands in his pockets.
Han satte hatt**en** på huvud**et.**	He put his hat on his head.
De förlorade minn**et.**	They lost their memories.
Hon bröt ben**et** av sig.	She broke her leg.

151 In some cases the English Possessive Adjective has no exact equivalent in Swedish.

Jag ber om ursäkt.	I beg your pardon.
Han har ändrat sig.	He has changed his mind.
Jag har gått vilse.	I have lost my way.

94

NON-NEUTER		NEUTER		PLURAL		
den [dɛn]	that	**det** [de:/t/]		**de**		those
denna [dɛ'na`]	this	**detta** [dɛ'ta`]		**dessa** [dɛ'sa`]		these
den där[1]	that	**det där**[1]		**de där**[1]		those
den här[2]	this	**det här**[2]		**de här**[2]		these

Den /där/ gossen är inte så dum, som han ser ut.	That boy is not so stupid as he looks.
Det svaret tycker jag om.	I like that answer.
De barnen[3] har aldrig gått i skola.	Those children have never been to school.
Denna uppgift är inte riktig.	This statement is not correct.
Dessa elever är längre komna än de andra.	These pupils are more advanced than the others.
Den här tavlan är vackrare än **den där**.	This picture is prettier than that.
Det där trädet är högre än **det här**.	That tree is taller than this /one/.
De här skorna är inte så bekväma som **de där**.	These shoes are not so comfortable as those.

Remarks on *den, denna, den här, den där*   153

(a) **Den, det, de,** are also used as the Definite Article of the Adjective. As Demonstratives they have stronger stress. Cf. §§ 78 and 165.

(b) The form *denne* (instead of *denna*) is often used when referring to a masculine noun.

(c) *Denna, detta, dessa* are literary forms. In conversation *den (det, de) här* and *den (det, de) där* are more usual. Colloquially *de här, de där* are pronounced [dɔm hæ:'r, dɔm dæ:'r].

---

[1] The stress is on *där*.
[2] The stress is on *här*.
[3] Coll. pronunciation: [dɔ'm bɑ:'ɳa`].

154 A noun qualified by *denna* (*detta, dessa*) does not take the definite terminal article, e. g. *denna dag* 'this day'; *detta hotell* 'this hotel'; *dessa städer* 'these towns'. Cf. § 83 *d*.

155 A noun qualified by *den, den här, den där* (and their inflected forms) takes the terminal definite article, e. g. *den dagen* 'that day'; *det hotellet* 'that hotel'; *de böckerna* 'those books'; *den här tavlan* 'this picture'; *det här hotellet* 'this hotel'; *de här tavlorna* 'these pictures'; *den där pojken* 'that boy'; *det där huset* 'that house'; *de där möblerna* 'that furniture'.

156 The demonstratives are often used as nouns, referring both to things and persons. When used as nouns *denne, detta, dessa* take the ending **-s** in the genitive.

Det var **det** jag sa'.	That's what I said.
Den är det.	That's the one.
Det (*or:* **Detta**) visste jag förut.	This (That) I knew before.
Jag vill inte ha **den här**. Ge mig **den där** i stället.	I don't want *this one*. Give me *that one* instead.
Denne är oskyldig.	*This man* is innocent.
Han frågade hennes advokat om saken, men **denne** ville inte lämna några upplysningar.	He asked her solicitor about it, but *the latter* was not willing to give any information.
Dennes syster bodde i London.	*The latter's* sister lived in London.

NOTE. — (*a*) The English word 'one' in 'this one', 'that one' is not translated.

NOTE. — (*b*) The genitive *dennes*, abbreviated to *ds.*, is used in dates for 'inst.', 'of this month', e. g. *Tack för Ert brev av den 17:de ds.* 'Thanks for your letter of the 17th inst.'.

157 Where English uses 'this' (that, these, those) as the subject of the verb 'to be' with a following noun (singular or plural) in the predicate, Swedish uses **det här** (**det där, detta**), i. e. the neuter singular form, irrespective of the gender or number of the following noun.

Det här är min svägerska.	This is my sister-in-law.
Det där är hennes pojkar.	Those are her boys.
Vad är **det där** för människor?	What people are those?
Detta var de ord han använde.	Those were the words he used.

Note the following expressions of time, where English 'this' is ren- **158**
dered by a prepositional phrase in Swedish: *i år* 'this year'; *i som-*
mar 'this summer'; *i morse* [mɔ'ṣeˋ] 'this morning'; *i eftermiddag* 'this
afternoon'; *i dag om fjorton dar* 'this day fortnight'; *i dag åtta dar*
'this day week'; *i dag för åtta dar sedan* [sɛn] 'this day last week';
Cf. also *endera dagen* 'one of these days'.

Note the following expressions: **159**

Det var därför, som jag måste flytta.	That is why I had to leave.
Just därför.	That's why.
Det var på det sättet, han lycka-des göra det.	That is how he managed to do it.
Jag gjorde så här.	I did it like this.
Stirra inte så där!	Don't stare like that!
Herr den och den.	Mr So-and-so.
Vid den och den tiden.	At such and such a time.
På den och den platsen.	At such and such a place.

Densamma and samma   **160**

NON-NEUTER		NEUTER	PLURAL
densamma [dɛnsa'ma]	the same	**detsamma**	**desamma**
samma [sa'maˋ]	the same	**samma**	**samma**

NOTE. — The forms *densamme, samme* (instead of *densamma, samma*)
are often used when referring to masculine nouns.

Densamma, detsamma, desamma are used as **Nouns.** They take the **161**
ending **-s** in the genitive.

Samma is used as an indeclinable **Adjective.**

Han är alltid **densamme.**	He is always the same.
Det gör mig alldeles **detsamma.**	It is all one to me.
Jag skall göra det **med det-samma.**	I will do it at once.
I detsamma fick han se läraren komma i dörren.	At that very moment he saw the master come in.
De kom på **samma** gång.	They arrived at the same time.
Han var klädd i **samma** gamla kostym.	He was wearing the same old suit.
I samma ögonblick dog han.	At that very moment he died.
Samma regler gäller även i detta fall.	The same rules apply in this case, too.

NOTE. — (*a*) After *samma* the adjective takes the definite form, but the noun the indefinite form: *samma gamla kostym; samma gröna färg* 'the same green colour'. Cf. § 87.

NOTE. — (*b*) No article is used before *samma: på samma sätt* 'in the same way'.

162 Sådan. Dylik

NON-NEUTER	NEUTER	PLURAL
/en/ **sådan** [so:'da`n] such	/ett/ **sådant**	**sådana**
/en/ **dylik** [dy:'li:'k] such	/ett/ **dylikt**	**dylika**

Sådan and *dylik* are used both as Adjectives and Nouns. The indefinite article (*en, ett*) is placed **before** *sådan* and *dylik*, not after as in English: *en sådan man* 'such a man'; *ett sådant exempel* 'such an example'.

Det där var en stilig båt. **En sådan** skulle jag vilja ha.	That is a fine boat. I should like to have one like it.
Sådant händer.	These (Such) things will happen.
I sådant (*or:* I så) fall.	In that case.

98

Sådan herre, **sådan** dräng.	Like master, like man.
Sådana finns det gott om.	There are plenty of those.
Ge mig fem **sådana**[1] **här**!	Give me five of these.
Något **dylikt** har jag aldrig hört.	I have never heard anything like it.
Han menade nog något **dylikt.**	I suppose he meant something like that.
Sådana ord som »här», »där», »hit», »dit», »nu», »då» **o. d.** (**och dylika**) kallas adverb.	Such words as 'here', 'there', 'hither', 'thither', 'now', 'then', etc., are called Adverbs.
Dylika metoder är inte att rekommendera.	Such methods are not to be recommended.

Sådan is also used in **exclamations.**   **163**

Ett **sådant**[2] barn han är!	What a child he is!
En **sådan** härlig utsikt!	What a splendid view!

EMPHASIZING PRONOUN AND ADJECTIVE   **164**

Själv

When the words 'myself', 'yourself', 'himself', etc., are used to emphasize the word (pronoun or noun) to which they refer, they are rendered by the Swedish **själv** [ʂɛlv], neuter **självt,** plural **själva.**

Han gjorde det **själv.**	He did it himself.
Låt dem göra det **själva.**	Let them do it themselves.
Nej, tänkte jag för **mig själv,** jag skall inte göra det.	No, I thought to myself, I will not do it.
Det skadar bara **honom själv** och ingen annan.	It only hurts *him* and no one else.
Han överträffade **sig själv.**	He surpassed himself.
Vi kan göra det **själva.**	We can do it ourselves.

---

[1] Coll. pronunciation: [sɔna].
[2] Coll. pronunciation: [sɔnt].

Jag kan laga till mitt te **själv**.	I can make my own tea.
Hon skulle aldrig ha tänkt på det **själv**.	She would never have thought of it herself.
Själva kungen.	The King himself.
I **själva** London.	In London itself.

165 DETERMINATIVE ADJECTIVE AND PRONOUN

Den, det, de are also used as Determinative Adjectives and Pronouns referring to a following relative clause, a prepositional phrase or an Infinitive. When used as Determinatives these words are always stressed. Cf. §§ 78 and 152.

Den[1] tavla, jag menar, är inte **den** ni tänker på.	The picture I mean is not the one you are thinking of.
Även **den,** som har gott om pengar, kan misslyckas vid försöket.	Even the man who has plenty of money may fail in the attempt.
Jag kunde inte få reda på **det** /som/ jag ville veta.	I could not find out what I wanted to know.
De[1] elever [ɛleːˈvɔr], som önskar stanna hemma, får göra det.	Those pupils who wish to stay at home may do so.
Stockholm och Göteborg är **de**[1] städer, som jag känner bäst till.	Stockholm and Gothenburg are the towns that I know best.
Det[1] hus, som ni ville köpa, är redan sålt.	The house you wanted to buy has already been sold.
Det här kaffet är starkare än **det,** som ni bjöd på i går.	This coffee is stronger than that which you gave us yesterday.
De som bor i glashus bör inte kasta sten.	Those who live in glass houses should not throw stones.
Den /av er/ som kommer först ska få en shilling.	The one /of you/ who comes first shall have a shilling.
Menar ni den här stolen eller **den** i hörnet?	Do you mean this chair or the one in the corner?

---

[1] Stressed.

When nouns in the plural are preceded by the Determinative Adjective, they do not take the terminal definite article: *de elever, som* ... (not: *de eleverna*). Nouns in the singular fluctuate. **166**

If used as a Noun the Determinative has the form **dem** (instead of **167** **de**) in the objective plural.

Han kände inte ens igen **dem**[1], som hade skött honom under hans sjukdom.	He did not even recognize those who had nursed him during his illness.
Jag gav pengarna till **dem,** som bäst behövde dem.	I gave the money to those who were most in need of it.

Den, det, de used as Demonstrative and Determinative Pronouns **168** (or Adjectives) are always stressed. Cf. §§ 78 and 152.

Den, det, de used as the Definite Article of the Adjective are always unstressed: *den lilla flickan, de små barnen,* etc.

No determinative pronoun is used in Swedish before a following **169** noun in the genitive.

Järnets smältpunkt är högre än kopparns.	The melting-point of iron is higher than *that of* copper.
Engelska fönster är olika andra länders.	English windows are different from *those of* other countries.

RELATIVE PRONOUNS   170

som (indeclinable)	who, which, that
vars (only genitive)	whose, of which
vad (indeclinable, only neuter)	what, that
vilken, neuter: **vilket**;	
plural (both genders): **vilka**	who, that, which.

---

[1] Stressed.

171 **Som** is the commonest relative pronoun and practically the only one used in conversation. It may be used for both genders, singular and plural. It is not used in the genitive or with a preceding preposition (Cf. §§ 173—174).

Jag såg en polis [pʊliːˈs], **som** hade arresterat en tjuv.	I saw a policeman who had arrested a thief.
Jag hittade boken, **som** jag hade tappat.	I found the book which I had lost.
De som är intresserade av historia bör läsa boken.	Those who are interested in history ought to read the book.
Han gav bort alla /de/ böcker, /**som**/ han hade köpt.	He gave away all the books he had bought.
Trädet, **som** ni ser där borta, är en palm.	The tree you see over there is a palm.

172 If *som* has to be used in connection with a preposition, the preposition is placed at the end of the relative clause, never before **som**. (Cf. § 174.)

Jag känner inte den person, /**som**/ ni talar **om**.	I don't know the person you are speaking of.

173 Instead of the missing genitive of *som* the genitives *vars*[1] or *vilkens* (*vilkets, vilkas*) may be used. (See § 175.) The genitives, however, are avoided in conversation.

Han är en man, på **vars** (*or:* vilkens) ord man kan lita.	He is a man on whose words you can rely.
De är män, på **vilkas** ord man kan lita.	They are men on whose words you can rely.

174 **Vilken, vilket, vilka** take an **-s** in the genitive. They may be preceded by a preposition.

---

[1] *Vars* refers to an antecedent in the singular; *vilkas* refers to an antecedent in the plural.

Där fanns höga stänger, **på vilka** nät hängde för att torka.	There were high poles on which nets were hanging to dry.
Den nya eleven [ɛle:'vən], **om vilken** jag talade, var också där.	The new pupil of whom I was speaking was there too.

Vars replaces the missing genitives of *som* and *vad*. It may be **175** preceded by a preposition. Cf. § 173.

Valet, *på* **vars** (*or* **vilkets**) *utgång* så mycket berodde, var ovanligt livligt.	The election, on the result of which so much depended, was exceptionally lively.

As object the Relative Pronoun is often omitted, though not to the **176** same extent as in English.

Den person du tänker på, är inte den jag menar.	The person you are thinking of is not the one I mean.

After *ingen, någon, sådan, samma,* and after a Superlative, *som* must be **177** used (not *vilken* or *vad*).

Som after *sådan* and *samma* corresponds to English 'as'.

Ingen, som en gång har sett det, kan någonsin glömma det.	Nobody who has seen it once can ever forget it.
Jag har **samma** elever, **som** jag hade förra året.	I have the same pupils as I had last year.
Jag köpte **den minsta, som** fanns.	I bought the smallest one there was.

When English relative 'which' refers back to a whole clause or a **178** word standing in the predicate, it is rendered by the neuter form *vilket* (not *som* or *vad*).

Han säger, att jag gör snabba framsteg, **vilket** gläder mig.	He says that I am making rapid progress, which I am glad to hear.
Jag trodde, att han låg sjuk, **vilket** han inte gjorde.	I thought that he was ill in bed, which he was not.

When English relative 'which' is used adjectivally (as an epithet),
it is rendered by *vilken* (*vilket, vilka*).

Han kommer nog att fråga mig, om jag vill följa med honom till Frankrike, i **vilket** fall jag tänker svara nej.	I am sure he will ask me if I should like to accompany him to France, in which case I am going to answer 'no'.

179 *Vad* is used in the sense of 'that which' and when the antecedent is
allt 'everything'.

Uppskjut inte till morgondagen, **vad** du kan göra i dag.	Do not put off till tomorrow what you can do today.
Han lyckas i **allt, vad** han företar sig.	He succeeds in everything he undertakes.

180 INDEFINITE RELATIVE PRONOUNS

vem som helst som	whoever
vem än	whoever
var och en som	whoever
vilken (**vilket, vilka**) **som helst som**	whoever, whatever, whichever
vad som helst som	whatever
vad än	whatever

De sålde sina varor till **vem som helst som** ville köpa dem.	They sold their wares to whoever would purchase them.
Vem ni **än** är, har ni inte rätt att vara här.	Whoever you are, you have no right to be here.
Vem som helst som hör honom tala måste beundra honom.	Whoever hears him speak must admire him.
Vad du /än/ gör, kom inte för sent till tåget!	Whatever you do, don't miss your train.
Vad som än händer.	Whatever happens.
Tag vilken/dera/ ni vill.	Take whichever you like.
Var och en som kommer är välkommen.	Whoever comes will be welcome.

INTERROGATIVE PRONOUNS AND ADJECTIVES   181

NON-NEUTER		NEUTER	PLURAL
vem [vɛm]	who, whom	vad [vɑ:/d/] what	—
vad för /en/	what /kind of/	vad för /ett/	vad för
		what /kind of/	/ena/
vilken	who, what, which	vilket	vilka
vilkendera	which /of them/	vilketdera	—
hurdan [hɯ:ˈḍaˈn] how, what/kind of/		hurdant	hurdana

Vem sa det?	Who said that?
Vem är den där mannen?	Who is that man?
Vilka är de där herrarna?	Who are those gentlemen?
Vem talar ni om?	Whom are you speaking about?
Vem träffade ni där	Whom did you meet there?
Vems glas är det här?	Whose glass is this?
Vad är det där?	What is that?
Vad har du gjort?	What have you done?
Vad i all världen gjorde du det för?	Whatever in the world did you do that for?
Vad för en bok vill ni ha? (or: Vad vill ni ha för en bok?)	What /kind of/ book will you have?
Vad för en pojke?	What boy?
Vad är det där för ett frimärke?	What stamp is that?
Vad är det där för frimärken?	What stamps are those?
Vad är det för slags karl?	What sort of a fellow is he?
Vad är ni för ena? (Coll.)	Who are you? (Plural.)
Vilken spårvagn skall jag ta?	Which tram do I take?
Vilket är ditt glas?	Which glass is yours?
Vilkens böcker är det där?	Whose books are those?
Vilka flaggor kan ni se på bilden?	What flags can you see in the picture?
Vilkendera tycker ni bäst om?	Which do you like best?
Hurdan hatt hade hon?	What kind of hat was she wearing?
Hurdant var vädret förra veckan?	What was the weather like last week?

105

NOTE. — (a) *Vem* refers only to **persons** and is not used adjectivally; it has the same form whether used as subject or object. The genitive form is *vems* 'whose'. The missing plural of *vem* is supplied by *vilka* 'who'.

NOTE. — (b) *Vad* is not used adjectivally.

NOTE. — (c) *Vilken* (*vilket, vilka*) and *vilkendera* (*vilketdera*) are used both as pronouns and adjectives. As pronouns they have the genitive forms *vilkens* (*vilkets, vilkas*), *vilkenderas* (*vilketderas*).

NOTE. — (d) *Vilken, vilket, vilka* are mostly used in a selecting sense ('which of . . .'), e. g. *Vilka /av er/ har varit i Sverige?* 'Which /of you/ have been in Sweden?' — The plural *vilka* corresponds to English 'what' when asking for a complete enumeration, e. g. **Vilka** *är de fyra årstiderna?* 'What are the four seasons?'

182 When the interrogative pronouns are used as **the subject in a dependent question,** they are followed by 'som'.

Jag vet, **vem som** har gjort det. I know who has done it.
Vet ni, **vad som** finns i den här Do you know what there is in lådan? this box?
Har ni hört, **vilka som** kom Have you heard who came first? först?
But: Jag vet inte, vem (vad, I don't know whom (what, vilka) han menar. which) he means

183 *Vilken* is also used in exclamations:

Vilken härlig utsikt! What a splendid view!
Vilket väder! What weather!

NOTE. — The indefinite article (*en, ett*) is not used after *vilken.*

184 Note the following expressions:

Hur ser hans far ut? What does his father look like?
Hur är det fatt? (Vad **är** det?) What is the matter?
Vilket är det ena, och vilket är Which is which? det andra?

106

INDEFINITE PRONOUNS AND ADJECTIVES

185

NON-NEUTER		NEUTER	PLURAL
man [man] one (gen. **ens,** objective **en**) (Cf. § 187)		— —	— —
någon	some, somebody (any, anybody)[1]	**något** some, something	**några**
ingen	no, nobody, none[1]	**inget, intet**	**inga**
somlig [sɔ'mli`g] some		**somligt**	**somliga**
annan [a'na`n] other, else		**annat**	**andra**
den andra the other		**det andra**	**de andra**
all	all	**allt**	**alla**
mången [mɔ'ŋə`n] many, many a /one/		**månget**	**många**
— —		**någonting** something	— —
— —		**ingenting** nothing	— —
— —		**allting** everything	— —
var	every, each[2]	**vart** [vat]	— —
varje	every, each[2]	**varje**	— —
var och en everybody, each		**vart och ett**	— —
varannan [vara'na`n] every other		**vartannat**	**varandra** each other
varenda [varɛ'nda`] /**en**/ every /one/		**vartenda** /**ett**/	— —
— —		**lite** [li:'tə`] a little, some	**få** few[3]
— —			**flera** several
endera [ɛ'nde:'ra] (= *en av dem*) either		**ettdera**	— —
någondera (= *någon av dem*) some one, either		**någotdera**	— —
ingendera (= *ingen av dem*) no one, neither		**intetdera**	— —

[1] Cf. § 189. [2] Cf. § 188. [3] Cf. 190.

Någon hade talat om det för henne.	Somebody had told her about it.
Har **någon** varit här?	Has anybody been here?
Nej, jag har inte sett **någon.**	No, I haven't seen anybody.
Jag skall fråga **någon annan.**	I will ask somebody else.
Det var **några** vänner till mig.	They were some friends of mine.
Har ni sett **några** böcker här?	Have you seen any books here?
Jag har inte gjort **något (någonting**[1]**)** i dag.	I haven't done anything today.
Är det **något** te kvar i tekannan? — Nej, det är **inget** kvar. — Jo, det är **lite.**	Is there any tea left in the teapot? — No, there is none left. — Yes, there is some.
Någonting är bättre än **ingenting.**	Something is better than nothing.
Ingen /människa/ har någonsin sett **någonting**[1] dylikt.	Nobody has ever seen anything like it.
Jag har **ingen** sked, och han har **inget** glas.	I haven't got a spoon, and he hasn't got a glass.
Har ni **någon annan** bok att låna mig?	Have you got any other book to lend me?
En annan gång skall jag berätta **några** sagor.	Another time I will tell some stories.
Det här glaset är inte rent. Ge mig **ett annat!**	This tumbler is not clean. Give me another.
Ge mig **någonting**[1] **annat!**	Give me something else.
Jag har **ingenting annat** att bjuda på.	I have nothing else to offer you.
Därav blev **intet.**	Nothing came of it.
Somliga människor är rika, **andra** är fattiga.	Some people are rich, others are poor.
De andra pojkarna har gått och badat.	The other boys have gone to have a bathe.
Allt är inte guld, som glimmar.	All that glitters is not gold.
Vi måste **alla** dö.	We must all die.

---

[1] Coll. pronounced [nɔntiŋ] when unstressed.

Allt (**Allting**) har sin tid.	There's a time for everything.
Mången skulle önska, att han vore i ert ställe.	Many a one would wish that he were in your place.
Var åttonde dag.	Once a week.
Tåg går **var** tionde minut.	Trains leave every ten minutes.
Med **få** minuters mellanrum.	Every few minutes.
Varannan dag. Var tredje dag.	Every other day. Every third day.
Vartannat hus.	Every other house.
De hjälper **varandra**.	They help each other.
De bär **varandras** bördor.	They carry one another's burdens.
Varje människa (**Var och en**) har sina egendomligheter.	Everybody has his peculiarities.
Var och en vet, hur svårt det är.	Everybody knows how difficult it is.
Han har **få** vänner.	He has few friends.
Jag känner **några** av dem.	I know *a few* of them.
Han gav pojkarna **var sitt** äpple (*or:* ett äpple var).	He gave the boys an apple each.
De gick åt **var sitt** håll.	They went their several ways.
De satt på **var sin** sida av (*or:* om) bordet.	They were seated on either side of the table.
Kan jag få **lite** mera te?	May I have some more tea?
Han lyckades **på ett eller annat sätt**.	He managed somehow or other.
Om **någon** skulle knacka på dörren, så öppna inte!	If anybody should knock at the door, do not open it.
Det gamla spelet om »Envar».	The old play 'Everyman'.

NOTE. — When used as nouns, *någon, ingen, annan, envar,* and *mången,* take an **-s** in the genitive.

The plurals *somliga, alla* when used as nouns also take an **-s** in the genitive. The genitive of *var och en* is *vars och ens.*

Enligt **någras** (somligas, allas) mening.	According to some people's (everybody's) opinion.

109

186 The interrogative pronouns *vem, vad, vilken (vilket, vilka)* are made into indefinite pronouns by adding **som helst.**

vem som helst	anybody /you like/
vad som helst	anything /you like/
vilken som helst	any, anyone /you like/

NEUTER: vilket som helst
PLURAL: vilka som helst

Vem som helst kan göra det.	Anybody can do it.
Vad som helst duger.	Anything will do.
Han brukade titta in vid **vilken** tid på dagen **som helst.**	He used to look in at any time of the day.
Man kan ta **vilket** tåg **som helst.**	You can take any train.
Fråga **vem som helst!**	Ask anybody.
Tänk på ett tal **vilket som helst!**	Think of any number you like.
Tag **vilken som helst** av dessa böcker.	Take any one of these books.
Vilken buss ska jag ta? — Vilken som helst.	Which bus do I take? — Any bus.

REMARKS ON THE USE OF CERTAIN INDEFINITE PRONOUNS

187 Man

Man is more widely used than 'one' in English; often when English has 'you', 'we', 'they', 'people', or a passive construction.[1]

Man måste göra **sin** plikt.	One must do one's duty.
Man har rätt att försvara **sig.**	One has a right to defend oneself.
Man kan se slottet härifrån.	You can see the castle from here.
Man kan aldrig veta.	You never can tell (*or:* There is no knowing).

---

[1] Cf. French 'on'.

Man kan komma dit med tåg.	You can get there by train.
I Frankrike dricker **man** mer kaffe än te.	In France they drink more coffee than tea.
Man erkänner allmänt, att ...	It is generally acknowledged that ...
Varför svarar du inte, när **man** talar till dig?	Why don't you answer when people speak to you (*or:* when you are spoken to)?

NOTE. — *Man* only occurs as subject; the missing genitive and objective forms are supplied by *ens, en,* e. g. *ens egna barn* 'one's own children'; *det skär en i hjärtat* 'it cuts one to the heart'.

Var. Varje. Varenda. All 188

Var, varje, varenda and *all* are only used as adjectives. The corresponding noun-forms are *var och en, varenda en.*

The neuter and plural forms of *all*: **allt, alla** may be used as Nouns.

England väntar, att **var** man gör sin plikt.	England expects that every man will do his duty.
Det är någonting, som **varje** (**varenda**) människa borde veta.	It is something that everybody (every one) ought to know.
Det är någonting, som **var och en** (**varenda en**) borde veta.	
Det är någonting, som **alla** borde veta.	
Tag **vart och ett** för sig!	Take each by itself.
Han har misslyckats i **vartenda** fall.	He has failed in each and every case.
Han har **all** anledning att vara nöjd.	He has every reason to be satisfied.
Allt möjligt.	All sorts of things.
När **allt** kommer omkring.	After all.
En för **alla** och alla för en.	All for each and each for all.
På **allt** sätt.	In every way.

111

Åt **alla** håll.	In every direction.
Allt emellanåt.	Every now and then.
Han är **allt annat än** lycklig.	He is *anything but* happy.

NOTE. — English 'all the' (= the whole) is rendered by *hela*.

Den franska renässansens **hela**	All the refinement of the French
förfining.	renaissance.
Hela tiden. **Hela** dagen.	All the time. All /the/ day.

189 Någon and Ingen

Någon (*något*, *några*) and *ingen* (*inget*, *inga*) are used as both adjectives and pronouns. *Någonting*, *ingenting* (and *allting*) are only used as pronouns.

Någon (*något*, *några*, *någonting*) is used not only in affirmative sentences but also in negative and interrogative sentences (where English has 'any', 'anybody', 'anything').

Jag har **inga** pengar. Har ni **några**?	I have no money. Have you any?
Jag har inte **något** vin kvar. Har ni **något**?	I have no wine left. Have you any?
Kan ni låna mig ett lexikon? — Jag har **inget** (*or:* inte något).	Could you lend me a dictionary? — I haven't got one.
Han har **inga** släktingar, och hon har **inga** heller.	He has no relatives and she has none either.
Jag har inte sett **någon.**	I have not seen anybody.
Har ni sett **någon**?	Have you seen anybody?
Om ni har sett **någon.**	If you have seen anybody.
Någonting annat?	Anything else?

NOTE. — (*a*) 'No' ('none', 'nobody', 'nothing') is often rendered by *inte någon* (*inte något*, *inte några*, *inte någonting*).

NOTE. — (*b*) '**Any**' ('anybody', 'anything'), when used in an affirmative phrase, corresponds to **vilken** (*vilket*, *vilka*, *vad*) **som helst** in Swedish. Cf. § 186.

112

Vilken pojke **som helst** kan
göra det.
     Any boy can do that.

Vad som helst duger.
     Anything will do.

Köp **vilka** böcker **som helst!**
     Buy any books you like.

NOTE. — (c) When 'some' ('any') is used in a partitive sense (corresponding to the partitive article in French) it is, as a rule, not translated. Sometimes the word *lite* is used in this sense.

Får jag servera er **lite** grönsaker?
— Tack, jag har.
 May I help you to some vegetables? — I have *some*, thank you.

De hade kaffe med sig i en termosflaska.
 They had brought *some* coffee in a thermos flask.

NOTE. — (d) 'Somewhat' is translated by *något* or *tämligen*.

'Some' before a Numeral is translated by *ungefär* or *omkring*.

'Any' before a Comparative is not translated.

Beskrivningen är **något** överdriven.
 The description is somewhat exaggerated.

Han levde för **omkring** trehundra år sedan.
 He lived some 300 years ago.

Jag orkar inte äta mer.
 I couldn't eat any more.

De hann inte längre.
 They did not get any further.

Few, a few. Little, a little. More   190

'Few' is translated by *få;* 'a few' by *några.*
'Little' is translated by *föga;* 'a little' by *lite;* 'very little' by *mycket lite.*

Få har sett det.
 Few have seen it.

Jag har sett **några** /stycken/.
 I have seen a few /of them/.

Föga eller ingenting.
 Little or nothing.

Jag har mycket **lite** pengar.
 I have very little money.

Lite av varje.
 A little of everything.

Flera means 'several', 'many', and (in comparisons) 'more'.

På **fleras** begäran.	In response to many people's request.
Med flera (m. fl.).	And others (etc.).
Han har **flera** frimärken än du.	He has more stamps than you.

191 Note the following expressions:

Någonting gott 'something good'; *vi tycker om tennis båda två* 'both of us are (we are both) fond of tennis'; *man kan säga båda delarna (vilket som helst)* 'you can say either'; *en för mycket* 'one too many'; *mycket folk* 'many people'.

192 Annan (annat, andra)

|En| annan, |ett| annat, andra are used both as pronouns and adjectives. The definite forms are: *den andra[1], det andra, de andra*. When used as pronouns they take the ending -*s* in the genitive.

Jag skall göra det **en annan** gång (vid **ett annat** tillfälle).	I will do it another time (on another occasion).
De andra kom aldrig tillbaka.	The others never came back.
Han hade tagit **en annans** hatt.	He had taken another person's hat.
Andras pengar.	Other people's money.
Den enes död, **den andres**[1] bröd.	One man's meat is another's poison.
Den ena gick ut, och **den andra** stannade hemma.	One went out, and the other stayed at home.
Å **ena** sidan . . . å **andra** sidan.	On the one hand . . . on the other hand.

NOTE. — (*a*) *Annan* after another pronoun often corresponds to English 'else'.

Det har **någon annan** gjort.	Somebody else has done it.
Vilken annan kunde ha gjort det?	Who else could have done it?
Vad annat kunde ni vänta?	What else could you expect?

---

[1] *Den andre* is sometimes used (instead of *den andra*) when referring to a masculine noun.

114

NOTE. — (*b*) English 'another' is often used in the sense of 'one more', 'an additional', e. g. 'Would you like another cup of tea?' In that case it is translated by *'en till ('ett till')* : *Vill ni ha en kopp te till?*

Note the following expressions: **193**

Vem kunde det annars vara? 'Who else could it be?'; *häromdagen* 'the other day'; *endera dagen* 'one of these days'; *ett eller annat* 'something or other'; *på ett eller annat sätt* 'somehow or other'.

The Verb

AUXILIARY VERBS

Ha¹ 'have'   **194**

PRESENT

jag	**har** [hɑ:r]	I have
du	har	you have
ni	har	you have
han	har	he has
hon	har	she has
den	har	it has
det	har	it has
vi	har (ha²)	we have
ni	har (ha²)	you have
de	har (ha²)	they have

PAST

jag	**hade** [ha'də`]	I had
du	hade	
ni	hade	
han	hade, etc.	
vi	hade, etc.	

PRESENT PERFECT

jag (etc.) **har haft** [haft]
    I have had

PAST PERFECT

jag (etc.) **hade haft**
    I had had

FUTURE

jag **skall** [ska] **ha³**
du (etc.) skall ha

I shall have
you (etc.) will have

---

¹ The older form *hava* is sometimes used in literature. It is nearly always pronounced *ha*. Cf. § 11: 6.
² In literary style the plural is *ha* (from the older *hava*).
³ or: *jag* (etc.) *kommer att ha.* See § 247.

vi skall[1] ha   we shall have
de skall ha   they will have

FUTURE IN THE PAST (CONDITIONAL)

jag **skulle** [sku'lə`] **ha**   I should have
du (etc.) skulle ha   you (etc.) would have

INFINITIVE   IMPERATIVE

att ha/va/ to have   **ha/v/** have

PRESENT PARTICIPLE   PAST PARTICIPLE (See § 200)

havande [hɑ:'vandə`] having   **havd** [havd] had

SUPINE (See § 199)

haft [haft] had

195 In the written language the auxiliary *ha* (*har, hade*) in the Present Perfect and Past Perfect is often omitted in subordinate clauses.

Som jag icke /har/ **fått** svar på   As I have had no reply to my
mitt förra brev . . .   previous letter . . .
Om jag inte /hade/ **hunnit** med   If I had missed the steamer, I
ångbåten, hade jag tagit tåget.   should have taken the train.

196 Vara [vɑ:'ra`] 'be'

PRESENT			PAST		
jag		I am	jag		I was
du		you are	du		you were
ni		you are	ni		you were
han	**är** [æ:r, ɛ:]	he is	han	**var** [vɑ:r, vɑ:]	he was
hon		she is	hon		she was
den		it is	den		it was
det		it is	det		it was

---

[1] In literary style the plural is *skola* [skɔla]. See § 198 *a.*

116

vi		we are	vi		we were
ni	**är**[1]	you are	ni	**var**[2]	you were
de		they are	de		they were

PRESENT PERFECT

jag (etc.) **har varit** [vɑːˈriˋt]
I have been

PAST PERFECT

jag (etc.) **hade varit** I had been

FUTURE

jag (etc.) **skall vara**[3] I shall be

FUTURE IN THE PAST (CONDITIONAL)

ag (etc.) **skulle vara** I should be

IMPERATIVE

var be

PRESENT PARTICIPLE

varande [vɑːˈrandəˋ] being

INFINITIVE

att vara to be

SUPINE[4]

varit been

Subjunctive

jag **vare** [vɑːˈrəˋ] I be
vi **vare** we be

jag **vore** [vɔːˈrəˋ] I were
vi **vore** we were

Vara and bliva [bliːˈvaˋ][5]   197

The verb *vara* denotes a **state** = 'be'.
The verb *bli/va/* denotes **transition** from one state to another =
'become', 'get'. Cf. § 230.

Det **är** mörkt.	It is dark.
Det börjar **bli** mörkt.	It is getting dark.

[1] In the written language (high style) the form *äro* [æːˈroˋ] is used in the plural: *vi (ni, de) äro.* Cf. § 11: 11.
[2] In the written language (high style) the form *voro* [vɔːˈroˋ] is used in the plural: *vi (ni, de) voro.*
[3] or: *jag kommer att vara.* See § 247.
[4] See § 199.
[5] In the spoken language the shortened form *bli* is used. Principal parts: *jag blir* 'I become', *blev* 'became', *har blivit* 'have become'. (See § 214.)

Det **blir** mörkt om en liten stund.	It will be dark in a little while.
Han **var** rädd för sin far.	He was afraid of his father.
Han **blev** rädd, när han hörde visselpipan.	He was (became) frightened when he heard the whistle.
De kommer att **vara** borta hela sommaren.	They will be away the whole summer.
Det ska **bli** roligt att träffa dem igen.	I am looking forward to seeing them again.
Vad tänker du **bli,** när du **blir** stor?	What are you going to be when you grow up?
Han **blev** dödad i kriget.	He was killed in the war.
När jag kom, **var** han redan död.	When I came, he was already dead.
Hennes mor har länge **varit** sjuk.	Her mother has long been ill.
I förra veckan **blev** hon opererad, och sedan dess har hon **blivit** bättre och bättre för var dag.	Last week she was operated on, and since then she has become better and better every day.
Han **blir** mer och mer lik sin far för varje år.	He is growing more and more like his father every year.

198 OTHER AUXILIARY VERBS

PRESENT		PAST	
(a) jag **skall** vi **skall**[1]	shall, will	**skulle**	should, would
(b) jag **vill** vi **vill**[1]	will, want to	**ville**	would, wanted to
(c) jag **kan** vi **kan**[1]	can	**kunde**	could, was able

INFINITIVE		SUPINE
att **skola**	to be obliged	**skolat**
att **vilja**	to be willing	**velat**
att **kunna**	to be able	**kunnat**

[1] In the written language the forms *skola* [skɔːˈlaˋ], *vilja* [viˈljaˋ], *kunna* [kuˈnaˋ] are often used in the plural.

(d) jag **måste** I must   **måste** had to
    vi **måste** we must

(e) jag **må**   I may   **måtte** may, might
    vi **må**

(f) jag **bör** I ought to ⎱
                              ⎰ see § 207
(g) jag **tör** I may   ⎰

VERBS WITH FULL MEANING

The Principal Parts of the Verb are:
Infinitive, Present, Past, Supine, and *Past Participle.*

Supine (Cf. § 275)   199

The Supine is the form of the Verb used after the auxiliary verb
ha (har, hade) 'have', in compound tenses, e. g.:

jag har **kallat**   I have called
jag hade **kallat** I had called
att ha **kallat**   to have called

Past Participle (Cf. § 274)   200

The Swedish Past Participle, on the other hand, is never used to
form the Present Perfect or the Past Perfect. The Swedish Past
Participle is used after the auxiliary verbs *vara (är, var, varit)* 'be',
and *bli (blir, blev, blivit)* 'become', and as an Adjective, e. g.:

jag är (var) **kallad**   I am (was) called
jag blev (har blivit) **kallad** I was (have been) called
att bli **kallad**   to be called

Consequently there are two forms in Swedish (Supine and Past
Part.) which correspond to the English Past Participle.

201 CONJUGATIONS

There are in Swedish **four Conjugations,** distinguished by the form of the **Supine.**

In the 1st Conjugation the Supine ends in **-at.**
In the 2nd Conjugation the Supine ends in **-t.**
In the 3rd Conjugation the Supine ends in **-tt.**
In the 4th Conjugation the Supine ends in **-it.**

202 FIRST CONJUGATION

Supine ends in **-at.**
Past ends in **-ade.**

EXAMPLE: **kalla** [ka'la'] 'call'

PRESENT	PAST
jag **kallar**¹ [ka'la'r] I call	jag **kallade**² [ka'ladə'] I called
PRESENT PERFECT	PAST PERFECT
jag **har kallat** I have called	jag **hade kallat** I had called
FUTURE	FUTURE IN THE PAST
jag **skall kalla**³ I shall call	jag **skulle kalla** I should call

IMPERATIVE: **kalla** call

INFINITIVE: **att kalla** to call

PRESENT PARTICIPLE: **kallande** [ka'landə'] calling

PAST PARTICIPLE: **kallad** [ka'la'd] called
(den är kall**ad,** det är kall**at,** de är kall**ade**)
Cf. § 220.

SUPINE: (jag har) **kallat** [ka'la't] called

---

¹ The same form for all persons, singular and plural. In elevated literary style the present plural drops the **-r** termination, i. e. it is like the infinitive: *vi (ni, de) kalla* 'we (you, they) call'. Cf. § 11: 6.
² The same form throughout.
³ or: *jag kommer att kalla.* See § 247.

120

The majority of Swedish verbs belong to the First Conjugation

It includes all verbs of foreign origin ending in **-era,** e. g. *studera* 'to study'; *fotografera* 'to take photographs'. Verbs in **-era** and verbs beginning with the prefixes **be-** or **för-** have Tone I, the others have Tone II. See § 6 *f—g*.

EXAMPLES:

INFINITIVE	PRESENT	PAST	SUPINE	PAST PART.
dans**a** 'dance'	dans**ar**	dans**ade**	dans**at**	dans**ad**
bad**a** 'bathe'	bad**ar**	bad**ade**	bad**at**	bad**ad**
hopp**a** 'jump'	hopp**ar**	hopp**ade**	hopp**at**	/över/hopp**ad**
telefoner**a** 'telephone'	telefoner**ar**	telefoner**ade**	telefoner**at**	telefoner**ad**

Negative and Interrogative Forms   203

Swedish has no equivalent of the English periphrastic constructions with 'do' (does, did) in negative and interrogative sentences. Compare:

Jag talar svenska.	I speak Swedish.
Jag **talar inte**[1] svenska.	I do not speak Swedish.
Talar er mor svenska?	Does your mother speak Swedish?
Hon **talar inte** svenska.	She does not speak Swedish.
Tala inte engelska!	Do not speak English.
Han **talade inte** engelska.	He did not speak English.
Talade han inte engelska?	Did he not speak English?

---

[1] In literature *icke* or *ej*.

204 SECOND CONJUGATION

Supine ends in **-t.**

The verbs of the Second Conjugation are divided into two classes according to whether the root ends in a **voiced** consonant (First Class) or a **voiceless** consonant (Second Class).

(a) First Class

Past tense ends in **-de.**
Past participle ends in **-d.**

EXAMPLE: **böja** [bœ'ja`] 'bend'

PRESENT

jag **böjer**[1] [bœ'jər] I bend

PAST

jag **böjde**[1] [bœ'jdə`] I bent

PRESENT PERFECT

jag **har böjt** I have bent

PAST PERFECT

jag **hade böjt** I had bent

FUTURE

jag **skall böja** I shall bend

FUTURE IN THE PAST

jag **skulle böja** I should bend

IMPERATIVE: **böj**   bend

INFINITIVE: **att böja** [bœ'ja`]   to bend

PRESENT PARTICIPLE: **böjande** [bœ'jandə`][2] bending

PAST PARTICIPLE: **böjd**   bent
(den är böj**d**, det är böj**t**, de är böj**da**).

SUPINE: (jag har) **böjt**   bent

---

[1] The Present Tense has Tone I. The Past Tense has Tone II. In the written language the preseet plural often ends in **-a** like the Infinitive: vi (ni, de) böja [bœ'ja`].
[2] The Present Participle is formed by adding **-nde** to the Infinitive, e. g. brännande. — The Imperative is formed by dropping the **-a** of the Infinitive, e. g. vänd!

122

EXAMPLES:

INFINITIVE	PRESENT	PAST	SUPINE	PAST PART.[1]
sända	sänder	sände[2]	sänt[2]	sänd[2]
'send'				
vända	vänder	vände[2]	vänt[2]	vänd[2]
'turn'				
gömma	gömmer	gömde[3]	gömt[3]	gömd[3]
'hide'				
ställa	ställer	ställde	ställt	ställd
'put'				
känna	känner	kände[3]	känt[3]	känd[3]
'feel', 'know'				
bränna	bränner	brände[3]	bränt[3]	bränd[3]
'burn'				
leda	leder	ledde[4]	lett	ledd
'lead'				
betyda[5]	betyder	betydde	betytt	— —
'mean', 'denote'				

NOTE. — (a) To the First Class belong verbs the root of which ends in a voiced[6] consonant.

NOTE. — (b) When the root ends in **-r**, the termination **-er** in the present tense is dropped, e. g.:

höra 'hear'	hör	hörde	hört	hörd
[hə:'ra`]	[hə:r]	[hə:'də`]	[hə:ţ]	[hə:ḑ]
röra	rör	rörde	rört	rörd
'move'				

---

[1] See note 2 p. 122.

[2] When the root ends in **-nd**, the **-d** is dropped before the **-d** or **-t** of the past forms.

[3] When the root ends in **-mm** or **-nn**, the double consonant is simplified in the past forms. — In the Imperative the double **n** is retained, e. g. *känn!*; but the double **m** is simplified, e. g. *göm!*

[4] When the root-vowel is long and followed by a **d**, the Past, Supine and Past Part. have short vowel and double consonant.

[5] Verbs with the prefix **be-** have Tone I (see § 6 f—g).

[6] All the consonants are voiced except *k, p, s, t*, which are voiceless.

123

INFINITIVE	PRESENT	PAST	SUPINE	PAST PART.
köra [çɘ:'ra'] 'drive'	kör	körde	kört	körd
lära 'teach', 'learn'	lär	lärde	lärt	lärd

(b) **Second Class**

Past tense ends in **-te.**

Past participle ends in **-t.**

EXAMPLE: **köpa** [çø:'pa'] 'buy'

PRESENT

jag **köper** [çø:'pər] I buy

PAST

jag **köpte** [çø:'ptə'] I bought

PRESENT PERFECT

jag **har köpt** I have bought

PAST PERFECT

jag **hade köpt** I had bought

FUTURE

jag **skall köpa** I shall buy

FUTURE IN THE PAST

jag **skulle köpa** I should buy

IMPERATIVE: **köp** buy

INFINITIVE: **att köpa** [çø:'pa'] to buy

PRESENT PARTICIPLE: **köpande** [çø:'pandə'] buying

PAST PARTICIPLE: **köpt** [çø:pt] bought
(den är köpt, det är köpt, de är köpta)

SUPINE: (jag har) **köpt** [çø:pt] bought

EXAMPLES:

INFINITIVE	PRESENT	PAST	SUPINE	PAST PART.
läsa [lɛ:'sa'] 'read'	läser [lɛ:'sər]	läste [lɛ:'stə']	läst [lɛ:st]	läst

124

INFINITIVE	PRESENT	PAST	SUPINE	PAST PART.
söka	söker	sökte	sökt	sökt
'seek'		[sø:'ktə`]	[sø:kt]	
tänka	tänker	tänkte	tänkt	tänkt
'think'				
tycka	tycker	tyckte	tyckt	tyckt
'think'				
leka	leker	lekte	lekt	lekt
'play'		[le:'ktə]	[le:kt]	
smälta	smälter	smälte	smält	smält
'melt'				

NOTE. — (*a*) To the Second Class belong verbs the root of which ends in **k, p, s** or **t** (voiceless consonants).

NOTE. — (*b*) When the root ends in **-t,** preceded by a long vowel, the Past, the Supine, and the Past Part. have double **-t** and short vowel, e. g.:

möta	möter	mötte	mött	mött
'meet'		[mœ'tə`]		
mäta	mäter	mätte	mätt	mätt
'measure'		[mɛ'tə`]		

Nearly all verbs of the Second Conjugation have **a soft vowel** (**e, i, y, ä, ö**) in the root (EXCEPTIONS: *gnaga* 'gnaw'; *åka* 'drive, go'; *blåsa* 'blow'; *befalla* 'command').

THIRD CONJUGATION

Supine ends in **-tt.**
Past ends in **-dde.**

EXAMPLE: **bo** [bω:] 'dwell'

PRESENT	PAST
jag **bor**[1] [bω:r] I dwell, live	jag **bodde** [bω'də`] I dwelt

---

[1] In elevated literary style the present plural has the form of the infinitive: *vi* (*ni, de*) *bo* [bω:]; *vi tro; vi sy,* etc.

PRESENT PERFECT	PAST PERFECT
jag **har bott** [bʊt] I have dwelt	jag **hade bott** I had dwelt
FUTURE	FUTURE IN THE PAST
jag **skall bo** I shall dwell	jag **skulle bo** I should dwell

IMPERATIVE:	**bo** [bω:]	dwell
INFINITIVE:	**att bo**	to dwell
PRESENT PARTICIPLE:	**boende** [bω:'əndə'] dwelling	
PAST PARTICIPLE:	(**bebodd** [bəbω'd] inhabited)	
	(neuter: bebo**tt,** pl. bebo**dda**). Se § 220.	
SUPINE:	(jag har) **bott**	dwelt

EXAMPLES:

INFINITIVE	PRESENT	PAST	SUPINE	PAST PART.[2]
tro [trω:]	tro**r**[1]	tro**dde**	tro**tt**	tro**dd**
'believe'	[trω:r]	[trω'də']	[trωt]	
ro	ro**r**[1]	ro**dde**	ro**tt**	ro**dd**
'row'				
sy	sy**r**[1]	sy**dde**	sy**tt**	sy**dd**
'sew'				
fly	fly**r**[1]	fly**dde**	fly**tt**	fly**dd**
'flee'				
klå [klo:]	klå**r**[1]	klå**dde**	klå**tt**	klå**dd**
'beat'		[klɔ'də']	[klɔt]	

Only a few verbs belong to the Third Conjugation. They are, as a rule, monosyllabic. The Infinitive and the (literary) Present plural do not take the usual ending **-a.**

206 Irregular Verbs of the First Conjugation

INFINITIVE	PRESENT	PAST	SUPINE
heta 'be called'	he**ter**[1] [he:'tər]	he**tte** [hɛ'tə']	he**tat** [he:'ta't]
kunna 'be able'	**kan**[1]	kun**de**	kunn**at**

---

[1] In literary elevated style the plural of the Present is like the Infinitive: *vi tro, vi sy, vi heta, vi kunna,* etc.

[2] The Present Participle is formed by adding **-ende** to the Infinitive, e. g. *troende, flyende* (Tone II). The Imperative is like the Infinitive, e. g. *tro! fly!*

126

leva 'live'	lever	levde [le:'vdə`]	levat
veta 'know'	**vet** [ve:t]	**visste**	vetat
vilja 'be willing'	**vill**	vi**lle**	**velat**

NOTE. — The supine of these verbs is formed according to the First Conjugation.

Irregular Verbs of the Second Conjugation 207

INFINITIVE	PRESENT	PAST	SUPINE	PAST PART.
böra	**bör**¹	borde	bort	
[bə:'ra`]		[bω:'də`]	[bω:ʈ]	
'ought to'				
dölja	döljer	dolde	dolt	dold
'conceal'		[do:'ldə`]	[do:lt]	
glädja [ɛ:]	gläder	gladde	glatt	
'gladden'				
göra	**gör**	gjorde	gjort	gjord
[jə:'ra`]		[jω:'də`]	[jω:ʈ]	
'do', 'make'				
lägga²	lägger	lade	lagt	lagd
'lay'			[lakt]	
skilja[ʂi'lja`]	skiljer	skilde	skilt	skild
'separate'				
smörja	smörjer	smorde	smort	smord
'lubricate'		[smω:'də`]	[smω:ʈ]	
spörja	spörjer	sporde	sport	spord
'ask'		[spω:'də`]	[spω:t]	
städja [ɛ:]	städjer	stadde	statt	stadd
'hire'				
stödja [ø:]	stöder	stödde [œ]	stött	stödd
'support'				
säga	säger	sade	sagt	sagd
[sɛ'ja`]	[sɛ'jər]	[sɑ:'/də`/]	[sakt]	
'say'				

¹ In literary elevated style the plural of the Present is like the Infinitive: *vi böra, vi glädja,* etc.

² Cf *ligga* § 214.

INFINITIVE	PRESENT	PAST	SUPINE	PAST PART.
sälja	säljer	sålde	sålt	såld
'sell'		[sɔ'ldə`]	[sɔlt]	
sätta	sätter	satte	satt	satt
'set'				
töras	**törs** [təṣ]	tordes	torts	
[tə:'ra`s]		[tω:'ḍə`s]	[tω:ʈṣ]	
'dare'				
(töra)	tör	torde [ω:]		
	'may'	'might'		
välja [ε]	väljer	valde	valt	vald
'choose'		[vɑ:'ldə`]	[vɑ:lt]	
vänja [ε]	vänjer	vande	vant	vand
'accustom'		[vɑ:'ndə`]	[vɑ:nt]	

208 Irregular Verbs of the Third Conjugation

INFINITIVE	PRESENT	PAST SING. (PLUR.[2])	SUPINE	PAST PART.
be/dja/[3]	ber[1]	**bad** (**bådo**)	bett	bedd
'ask', 'pray'	[be:r]	[bɑ:d]		
dö [dø:]	dör[1]	**dog** (**dogo**)	dött	(död)
'die'	[də:r]	[dω:g]		
få	får	**fick** (**fingo**)	fått	/and/fådd
'get', 'be allowed'				/lån/fången
gå	går	**gick** (**gingo**)	gått	**gången**
'go'		[jik]		[gɔ'ŋə`n]
le	ler	**log** (**logo**)	lett	/be/ledd
'smile'	[le:r]	[lω:g]		
se	ser	**såg** (**sågo**)	sett	sedd
'see'	[se:r]			
stå	står	**stod** (**stodo**)	stått	/för/stådd
'stand'		[ω:]		/över/**stånden**
slå	slår	See § 214.		
'strike'				

[1] In literary elevated style the plural of the Present is like the Infinitive.
[2] In the spoken language the singular forms are used throughout.
[3] The full form is used in elevated style, e. g. *Låtom oss bedja!* 'Let us pray!'

Supine ends in **-it.**
Past Participle ends in **-en.**

The Fourth Conjugation comprises the strong verbs. The Past is not formed by a termination as in the other conjugations but by **changing the root-vowel,** e. g. *binda,* Past *band,* Supine *bundit* [bu′ndi‵t].

The verbs of this conjugation are here classified according to the various vowel-changes.

Class I. Vowel-change: (short) **i—a—u**   210

EXAMPLE: **binda** [bi′nda‵] 'bind'

PRESENT		PAST	
jag **binder** [bin′dər] I bind		jag **band**	I bound
(vi **binda**¹	we bind)	(vi **bundo**¹ [bu′ndω‵]	we bound)

PRESENT PERFECT

jag **har bundit** I have bound

PAST PERFECT

jag **hade bundit** I had bound

FUTURE

jag **skall binda** I shall bind

FUTURE IN THE PAST

jag **skulle binda** I should bind

IMPERATIVE:	**bind**²	bind
INFINITIVE:	**att binda**	to bind
PRESENT PARTICIPLE:	**bindande**	binding
PAST PARTICIPLE:	**bunden** [bu′ndə‵n] bound	
	(det är) bund**et**, (de är) bund**na**	
SUPINE:	(jag har) **bundit** [bu′ndi‵t] bound	

¹ The plural forms are only used in elevated style. In the spoken language and in ordinary prose the singular forms are used throughout. Cf. § 11: 6.
² The Imperative is formed by dropping the **-a** of the Infinitive.

EXAMPLES:

INFINITIVE	PRESENT[1]	PAST SING.	(PLUR.[2])	SUPINE	PAST PART.
springa 'run'	springer	sprang	(sprungo)	sprungit	sprungen
finna 'find'	finner	fann	(funno)	funnit	funnen
brinna 'burn'	brinner	brann	(brunno)	brunnit	brunnen
dricka 'drink'	dricker	drack	(drucko)	druckit	drucken
rinna 'run', 'flow'	rinner	rann	(runno)	runnit	runnen
vinna 'win'	vinner	vann	(vunno)	vunnit	vunnen

211 Class II. Vowel-change: (long) **i — e — i**

PRESENT	PAST
jag **biter** I bite	jag **bet** [be:t] I bit
(vi **bita**[1] we bite)	(vi **beto**[2] we bit)

PRESENT PERFECT	PAST PERFECT
jag **har bitit** [bi:'tit`] I have bitten	jag **hade bitit** I had bitten

FUTURE	FUTURE IN THE PAST
jag **skall bita** I shall bite	jag **skulle bita** I should bite

IMPERATIVE:	**bit** [bi:t]	bite
INFINITIVE:	**att bita**	to bite
PRESENT PARTICIPLE:	**bitande**	biting
PAST PARTICIPLE:	**biten** [bi:'tə`n]	bitten
	(det är) bit**et**, (de är) bit**na**. Cf. § 220.
SUPINE:	(jag har) **bitit**	bitten

[1] In the spoken language the singular forms are used throughout. In elevated style the plural forms are like the Infinitive (*vi springa*, etc.).
[2] Only used in elevated style.

EXAMPLES:

INFINITIVE	PRESENT	PAST SING.	(PLUR.)	SUPINE	PAST PART.
skriva 'write'	skriver	skrev	(skrevo)	skrivit	skriven
gripa 'seize'	griper	grep	(grepo)	gripit	gripen
rida 'ride'	rider	red	(redo)	ridit	riden
bli/va/[1] 'become'	bli/ve/r[1]	blev	(blevo)	blivit	bliven
sprida 'spread'	sprider	spred	(spredo)	spritt[2]	spridd[2]
lida 'suffer'	lider	led	(ledo)	lidit	liden

Class III. Vowel-change: **y** (*or:* **ju**) — **ö** — **u** (**ju**)   212

PRESENT

jag **flyger** I fly

(vi **flyga** we fly)

PAST

jag **flög**   I flew

(vi **flögo** [flø:'gω`] we flew)

PRESENT PERFECT

jag **har flugit** [flɯ:'gi`t] I have flown

PAST PERFECT

jag **hade flugit** I had flown

FUTURE

jag **skall flyga** I shall fly

FUTURE IN THE PAST

jag **skulle flyga** I should fly

IMPERATIVE: **flyg**

INFINITIVE: **att flyga**

PRESENT PARTICIPLE: **flygande**

PAST PARTICIPLE: (den är) /bort/**flugen**
                    (det är) /bort/flug**et**, (de är) /bort/flug**na**

SUPINE: (jag har) **flugit**

---

[1] The full forms only used in elevated style.
[2] Irregular.

EXAMPLES:

INFINITIVE	PRESENT	PAST SING.	(PLUR.)	SUPINE	PAST PART.
frysa 'freeze'	fryser	frös	(fröso)	frusit	frusen
flyta 'float', 'flow'	flyter	flöt	(flöto)	flutit	/kring/fluten
krypa 'creep'	kryper	kröp	(kröpo)	krupit	krupen
bjuda 'offer'	bjuder	bjöd	(bjödo)	bjudit	bjuden
sjunga [ṣu'ŋaˋ] 'sing'	sjunger	sjöng	(sjöngo)	sjungit	sjungen
sjunka 'sink'	sjunker	sjönk	(sjönko)	sjunkit	sjunken
skjuta [ṣɯ:'taˋ] 'shoot'	skjuter	**sköt** [ṣø:t]	(sköto)	skjutit	skjuten

213 **Class IV.** Other Vowel Changes

INFINITIVE	PRESENT	PAST	SUPINE
(a) bära 'bear', 'carry'	bär	bar (buro)	burit
stjäla [ṣɛ:'laˋ] 'steal'	stjäl	stal (stulo)	stulit
skära [ṣæ:'raˋ] 'cut'	skär	skar [skɑ:r] (skuro)	skurit [sku:'riˋt]
(b) dra/ga/ 'draw', 'pull'	dra/ge/r	drog [drω:g] (drogo)	dragit[1]
ta/ga/ 'take'	ta/ge/r	tog [tω:g] (togo)	tagit[1]

---

[1] Present Participle: *dragande; tagande.* Imperative: *dra/g/; ta/g/.*

132

INFINITIVE	PRESENT	PAST	SUPINE
fara 'go'	far	for [fω:r] (foro)	farit
hålla 'hold'	håller	höll (höllo)	hållit
falla[1] 'fall'	faller	föll (föllo)	fallit

(c) ge (giva) [je:, ji:'va`] gav (gåvo) gett (givit)[2]
'give'

gråta 'weep'	gråter	grät (gräto)	gråtit
låta 'let'	låter	lät (läto)	låtit
komma 'come'		kom (kommo)	kommit
sova [so:'va`]	'sleep'	sov (sovo)	sovit
slå[3] 'strike'		slog [slω:g] (slogo)	slagit
svär/j/a 'swear'	svär	svor [svω:r] (svuro)	svurit
vara 'be'	är	var (voro)	varit
äta [ɛ:'ta`] 'eat'	äter	åt (åto)	ätit

ALPHABETICAL LIST OF STRONG VERBS 214

INFINITIVE	PRESENT	PAST SING.	(PLUR.)	SUPINE	PAST PART.[4]
binda 'bind'	binder	band	bundo	bundit	bunden
bita 'bite'	biter	bet	beto	bitit	biten

---

[1] *Befalla* [bəfa'la] 'command' is weak: *befalla — befallde — befallt.*
[2] Present Tense: *ger* [je:r] (*giver* [ji:'vər]). Present Participle: *givande.* Past Part. *given.* Imperative: *ge* (*giv*).
[3] Present Tense: *jag slår.*
[4] The Present Participle is formed by adding **-nde** to the Infinitive, e. g. *bindande.* The Imperative is formed by dropping the **-a** of the Infinitive, e. g. *bind! kom!* (one **m**).

133

INFINITIVE	PRESENT	PAST		SUPINE	PAST PART.
		SING.	PLUR.		
bjuda 'offer'	bjuder	bjöd	bjödo	bjudit	bjuden
bli/va/ 'become'	**blir**	blev	blevo	blivit	bliven
brinna 'burn'	brinner	brann	brunno	brunnit	brunnen
brista 'burst'	brister	brast	brusto	brustit	brusten
bryta 'break'	bryter	bröt	bröto	brutit	bruten
bära 'bear'	**bär**	bar	buro	burit	buren
dra/ga/ 'draw', 'pull'	dra/ge/r	drog	drogo	dragit	dragen
dricka 'drink'	dricker	drack	drucko	druckit	drucken
driva 'drive'	driver	drev	drevo	drivit	driven
falla 'fall'	faller	föll	föllo	fallit	fallen
fara 'go'	**far**	for [ω:]	foro	farit	/hädan/faren
finna 'find'	finner	fann	funno	funnit	funnen
flyga 'fly'	flyger	flög	flögo	flugit	/bort/flugen
flyta 'float'	flyter	flöt	flöto	flutit	fluten
frysa 'freeze'	fryser	frös	fröso	frusit	frusen
försvinna 'disappear'	försvinner	försvann	försvun- no	försvunnit	försvunnen
gala 'crow'	**gal**	gol [ω:]	golo	galit	—

134

INFINITIVE	PRESENT	PAST		SUPINE	PAST PART.
		SING.	PLUR.		
giva (ge) 'give'	giver (**ger**)	gav	gåvo	givit (gett)	given
gjuta [juː'ta`] 'cast', 'mould'	gjuter	göt [jøːt]	göto	gjutit	gjuten
glida 'glide'	glider	gled	gledo	glidit	—
gnida 'rub'	gnider	gned	gnedo	gnidit	gniden
gripa 'seize'	griper	grep	grepo	gripit	gripen
gråta 'weep'	gråter	grät [ɛ:]	gräto	gråtit	/be/gråten
hinna 'have time'	hinner	hann	hunno	hunnit	hunnen
hugga 'hew'	hugger	högg	höggo	huggit	huggen
hålla 'hold'	håller	höll	höllo	hållit	hållen
kliva 'stride'	kliver	klev	klevo	klivit	/upp/kliven
klyva 'cleave'	klyver	klöv	klövo	kluvit	kluven
knipa 'pinch'	kniper	knep	knepo	knipit	knipen
knyta 'tie'	knyter	knöt	knöto	knutit	knuten
komma 'come'	kommer	kom[1]	kommo	kommit	kommen
krypa 'creep'	kryper	kröp	kröpo	krupit	krupen

---

[1] One **m**! Also in the Imperative: *kom!*

INFINITIVE	PRESENT	PAST		SUPINE	PAST PART.
		SING.	PLUR.		
lida 'suffer'	lider	led	ledo	lidit	liden
ligga 'lie'	ligger	låg	lågo	**legat**	/för/**legad**
ljuda 'sound'	ljuder	ljöd	ljödo	ljudit	—
ljuga 'tell a lie'	ljuger	ljög	ljögo	ljugit	/be/ljugen
låta 'let'; 'sound'	låter	lät [ɛ:]	läto	låtit	/över/låten
niga 'curtsy'	niger	neg	nego	nigit	—
njuta 'enjoy'	njuter	njöt	njöto	njutit	njuten
pipa 'pipe'	piper	pep	pepo	pipit	—
rida 'ride'	rider	red	redo	ridit	riden
rinna 'run', 'flow'	rinner	rann	runno	runnit	runnen
riva 'tear'	river	rev	revo	rivit	riven
ryta 'roar'	ryter	röt	röto	rutit	ruten
sitta 'sit'	sitter	satt	sutto	suttit	/för/sutten
sjuda 'seethe'	sjuder	sjöd	sjödo	sjudit	sjuden
sjunga 'sing'	sjunger	sjöng	sjöngo	sjungit	sjungen
sjunka 'sink'	sjunker	sjönk	sjönko	sjunkit	sjunken
skina 'shine'	skiner	sken	skeno	skinit	—

INFINITIVE	PRESENT	PAST SING.	PLUR.	SUPINE	PAST PART.
skjuta 'shoot'	skjuter	sköt	sköto	skjutit	skjuten
skrida 'slide'	skrider	skred	skredo	skridit	/över/skri-den
skrika 'shriek'	skriker	skrek	skreko	skrikit	/ut/skriken
skriva 'write'	skriver	skrev	skrevo	skrivit	skriven
skryta 'boast'	skryter	skröt	skröto	skrutit	/om/skruten
skära 'cut'	**skär**	skar	skuro	skurit	skuren
slippa 'escape', 'be spared'	slipper	slapp	sluppo	sluppit	/upp/slup-pen
slita 'tear'	sliter	slet	sleto	slitit	sliten
sluta[1] 'conclude'	sluter	slöt	slöto	slutit	sluten
slå 'strike'	**slår**	slog	slogo	slagit	slagen
smyga 'slip'	smyger	smög	smögo	smugit	/in/smugen
snyta 'blow the nose'	snyter	snöt	snöto	snutit	/o/snuten
sova [o:] 'sleep'	sover	sov	sovo	sovit	—
spinna 'spin'	spinner	spann	spunno	spunnit	spunnen
spricka 'burst'	spricker	sprack	sprucko	spruckit	sprucken

---

[1] When *sluta* means 'finish', it is conjugated according to the 1st conjugation: *sluta — slutar — slutade — slutat — slutad.*

INFINITIVE	PRESENT	PAST SING.	PLUR.	SUPINE	PAST PART.
sprida 'spread'	sprider	spred¹	spredo¹	**spritt**	**spridd**
springa 'run'	springer	sprang	sprungo	sprungit	sprungen
spritta 'start up'	spritter	spratt	sprutto	—	—
sticka 'stick', 'prick'	sticker	stack	stucko	stuckit	stucken
stiga 'rise'	stiger	steg	stego	stigit	stigen
stjäla 'steal'	**stjäl**	stal	stulo	stulit	stulen
strida 'fight'	strider	stred²	stredo²	stridit³	/be/**stridd**
stryka 'stroke'	stryker	strök	ströko	strukit	struken
supa 'tipple'	super	söp	söpo	supit	/för/supen
svida 'smart'	svider	sved	svedo	svidit	—
svika 'betray'	sviker	svek	sveko	svikit	sviken
svär/j/a 'swear'	**svär** [ω:]	svor	svuro	svurit	svuren
ta/ga/ 'take'	ta/ge/r	tog	togo	tagit	tagen
tiga 'be silent'	tiger	teg	tego	**tegat**	/för/tegen
tjuta 'howl'	tjuter	tjöt	tjöto	tjutit	—

---

¹ also *spridde*.
² also *stridde*.
³ also *stritt*.

138

INFINITIVE	PRESENT	PAST		SUPINE	PAST PART.
		SING.	PLUR.		
vika 'fold'	viker	vek	veko	vikit[1]	viken[1]
vina 'whiz'	viner	ven	veno	vinit	—
vinna 'win'	vinner	vann	vunno	vunnit	vunnen
vrida 'twist'	vrider	vred	vredo	vridit	vriden
äta 'eat'	äter	åt	åto	ätit	äten

REMARKS ON THE TERMINATIONS OF THE VERB 215

The Infinitive

1st Conjugation: att tala, att kalla, att bada
2nd Conjugation: att böja, att köpa, att söka
3rd Conjugation: att bo, att sy, att få
4th Conjugation: att binda, att komma, att bita

The Infinitive ends in **-a,** except in the 3rd Conjugation where the Infinitive lacks the **-a** termination.

The Present 216

1st Conjugation: jag talar, jag kallar, jag badar
2nd Conjugation: jag böjer, jag köper, jag söker
3rd Conjugation: jag bor, jag syr, jag får
4th Conjugation: jag binder, jag kommer, jag biter

1st Conjugation: the Present singular ends in **-ar**
2nd Conjugation: the Present singular ends in **-er**
3rd Conjugation: the Present singular ends in **-r**
4th Conjugation: the Present singular ends in **-er**

---

[1] Also *vikt* [vi:kt].

139

The Present plural (which is only used in the written language) has the same form as the Infinitive, e. g. *vi tala; vi köpa; vi bo; vi binda.* EXCEPTION: vi **äro** 'we are' (Infinitive: *vara*).

217 The Past

1st Conjugation: jag tal**ade**, jag kall**ade**, jag bad**ade**
2nd Conjugation: jag böj**de**, jag köp**te**, jag sök**te**
3rd Conjugation: jag bo**dde**, jag tro**dde**, jag sy**dde**
4th Conjugation: jag band, jag kom, jag bet

1st Conjugation: the Past ends in **-ade**
2nd Conjugation: the Past ends in **-de** or **-te**
3rd Conjugation: the Past ends in **-dde**
4th Conjugation: the Past singular has no termination

The Past plural of the 1st, 2nd and 3rd Conjugations has the same form as the singular, both in the spoken and the written language.

The Past plural of the 4th Conjugation ends in **-o**, e. g. *vi bundo, vi kommo, vi beto*. The plural forms are only used in literature.

218 The Imperative

1st Conjugation: tal**a**! kall**a**! bad**a**!
2nd Conjugation: böj! köp! sök!
3rd Conjugation: bo! sy! gå!
4th Conjugation: bind! kom! bit!

1st and 3rd Conjugations: the Imperative has the same form as the Infinitive.
2nd and 4th Conjugations: the Imperative consists of the bare stem of the verb (i. e. it lacks the **-a** termination of the Infinitive).

219 The Supine

1st Conjugation: tal**at**, kall**at**, bad**at**
2nd Conjugation: böj**t**, köp**t**, sök**t**
3rd Conjugation: bo**tt**, sy**tt**, gå**tt**
4th Conjugation: bund**it**, komm**it**, bit**it**

140

1st Conjugation: the Supine ends in **-at**
2nd Conjugation: the Supine ends in **-t**
3rd Conjugation: the Supine ends in **-tt**
4th Conjugation: the Supine ends in **-it**
The Supine is indeclinable.

The Past Participle 220

The Past Participle of all the conjugations is declined like an ordinary **Adjective**. See § 76—83; 119—121.

	NON-NEUTER	NEUTER	PLURAL
1st Conjugation:	kall**ad**	kall**at**	kall**ade**
2nd Conjugation:	böj**d**	böj**t**	böj**da**
	köp**t**	köp**t**	köp**ta**
3rd Conjugation:	tro**dd**	tro**tt**	tro**dda**
4th Conjugation:	bund**en**	bund**et**	bund**na**

The Present Participle 221

1st Conjugation: tal**ande**, kall**ande**, bad**ande**
2nd Conjugation: böj**ande**, köp**ande**, sök**ande**
3rd Conjugation: bo**ende**, sy**ende**, gå**ende**
4th Conjugation: bind**ande**, komm**ande**, bit**ande**

1st, 2nd and 4th Conjugations: the Present Participle ends in **-ande**.
3rd Conjugation: the Present Participle ends in **-ende**.

NOTE. — When used as an adjective the Present Participle is indeclinable. See § 122. When used as a noun it is declined according to the 5th Declension. See §§ 70—72.

SUBJUNCTIVE 222

The special forms of the Subjunctive are gradually falling out of use in modern Swedish. Very few are retained in the spoken language. They all end in **-e**.

The **Present Subjunctive** is formed by changing the **-a** of the 223 Infinitive into **-e**.

INFINITIVE		PRESENT SUBJUNCTIVE
att leva	live	leve
välsigna	bless	välsigne
vara	be	vare
komma	come	komme

EXAMPLES:

Leve konungen!	Long live the King!
Gud **välsigne** dig!	God bless you!
Gud **vare** med dig!	God be with you!
Vare därmed hur som helst.	Be that as it may.
Rädde sig den som kan!	Let him save himself who can!
Ske Din vilja!	Thy will be done!

224 The **Past Subjunctive** of the 1st, 2nd and 3rd Conjugations is like the Past Indicative, e. g.: *talade, köpte, trodde.*

225 The **Past Subjunctive** of the 4th Conjugation is formed by changing the **-o** of the **plural** Past Indicative into **-e.**

PLURAL OF PAST INDICATIVE			PAST SUBJUNCTIVE	
(att giva)	vi gåv**o**	gave	jag gåv**e**	(vi gåve)
(att vinna)	vi vunn**o**	won	jag vunn**e**	(vi vunne)
(att vara)	vi vor**o**	were	jag vor**e**	(vi vore)
(att få)	vi fing**o**	got	jag fing**e**	(vi finge)

226 EXAMPLES showing the use of the Past Subjunctive:

Jag önskar, att det aldrig **bleve**[1] sommar!	I wish it would never be summer!
Om jag **vore** kung.	If I were king.
Om jag **finge**[1], **toge**[1] jag platsen genast.	If I were allowed, I would take the situation at once.
Om inte månen **funnes**[1], skulle det inte finnas något tidvatten.	If the moon did not exist, there would be no tide.

---

[1] In the spoken language the Indicative forms are preferred: *blev, fick, tog, fanns.*

The Passive is formed:

(*a*) *either* by using the auxiliary verb **bli** with the Past Participle of the main verb, e. g. *Han* **blev tagen** *till fånga* 'He was taken prisoner';

(*b*) *or* by adding **-s** to the active forms of the verb, e. g. *Han* **togs** *till fånga.*

If the active form ends in **-r,** this **-r** is dropped before the **-s** termination, e. g. *jag kallar,* passive *jag kalla***s**.

The periphrastic forms with *bli* (and *vara*) are treated in §§ 230—234.

s-Forms

1st Conjugation
228

PRESENT	PAST
jag **kallas** I am called	jag **kallades** I was called

PRESENT PERFECT	PAST PERFECT
jag **har kallats** I have been called	jag **hade kallats** I had been called

FUTURE	FUTURE IN THE PAST
jag **skall kallas** I shall be called	jag **skulle kallas** I should be called

INFINITIVE: **att kallas** to be called

SUPINE: **kallats** been called

(PAST PARTICIPLE: **kallad** called)

2nd, 3rd and 4th Conjugations

INFINITIVE		PRESENT		
att köpas	to be bought	**köp/e/s**	is bought	(pl. **köpas**[1])
att böjas	to be bent	**böj/e/s**	is bent	(**böjas**)
att tros	to be believed	**tros**	is believed	(**tros**)
att bindas	to be bound	**bind/e/s**	is bound	(**bindas**)
att brytas	to be broken	**bryt/e/s**	is broken	(**brytas**)

PAST		PRESENT PERFECT	
köptes	was bought	**har köpts**	has been bought
böjdes	was bent	**har böjts**	has been bent
troddes	was believed	**har trotts**	has been believed
bands	was bound (pl. **bundos**[1])	**har bundits**	has been bound
bröts	was broken (pl. **brötos**)	**har brutits**	has been broken

NOTE. — If the active form ends in **-er** (Present of the 2nd and 4th conjugations) the **-e-** is generally dropped before the **-s** termination (except in literary and formal style), e. g. *det köps; det böjs; det binds; det bryts; det känns* 'it is felt'; *det glöms* 'it is forgotten'.

230 Periphrastic Forms

The Passive Voice may also be formed by using the auxiliary verbs **bliva** or **vara** together with the Past Participle of the main verb.

Han **är älskad** av alla. ⎫
Han **älskas** av alla. ⎭ He is loved by everybody.

Han har **blivit vald** till riksdagsman. ⎫
Han har **valts** till riksdagsman ⎭ He has been elected a Member of Parliament.

231 Use of the Periphrastic Forms and the s-Forms

It is difficult to give any simple rules as to the use of the **s**-forms and the periphrastic forms.

---

[1] The plural forms are not used in the colloquial language.

In general it may be said that the Passive formed by the auxiliary *bli* with the Past Participle of the main verb is far more frequently used than the **s**-form, especially in the spoken language.

In order to know whether to use the periphrastic forms (with *bli* and *vara*) or the **s**-forms it is useful to distinguish between **verbs of transition** and **verbs of duration.**

Verbs of transition denote actions or processes which imply a change of state or lead to a cessation, e. g. *tända* 'light'; *flytta* 'remove'. Verbs of duration denote a continued action without reference to a change of state or to a cessation, e. g. *älska* 'love'; *frukta* 'fear'.

The Passive of Verbs of Transition 232

(*a*) Present Tense: the **s-form** implies customary or repeated actions or processes. It is therefore often used in public notices, advertisements, descriptions of processes (e. g. recipes), etc.

På julafton **tänd/a/s** ljusen i julgranen, och julklapparna **delas ut.**[1]	On Christmas Eve the Christmas-tree candles are lighted, and the Christmas gifts are distributed.
Supin [sɯpi:'n] **brukas** efter hjälpverbet 'ha'.	The Supine is used after the auxiliary verb 'to have'.
Avlagda kläder /**upp**/**köpas.**	Cast-off clothes bought.
Föremålen få icke /**vid**/**röras.**	Do not touch the exhibits!

(*b*) Past Tense: **s-forms** and periphrastic forms with **bli** are, as a rule, used without distinction.

Papperen **lades** åt sidan.
Papperen **blev lagda** åt si- } The papers were put aside.
dan.

NOTE. — Periphrastic forms with **vara** in the Present and the Past indicate completed action, the result of which still remains or remained.

---

[1] Compare: *Ljusen* **är tända** 'The candles **are alight**'; *Julklapparna* **är utdelade** 'The Christmas gifts **have been distributed**'.

145

Himlen **är täckt** av moln.	The sky is covered with clouds.
(Cf. Himlen **täck/e/s** av moln.	The sky *is getting overcast*.)
Bilen **var stulen.**	The car *had been stolen*.
(Cf. Bilen stals.	The car was stolen.)

(c) Present Perfect and Past Perfect: **s-forms** and periphrastic forms with **bli** denote completed action.

Bilen har (hade) **stulits.**	
Bilen har (hade) **blivit**[1] **stulen.**	The car has (had) been stolen.
Han hade **blivit**[1] **skjuten.**	He had been shot.

NOTE. — Periphrastic forms with **vara** in the Present Perfect and the Past Perfect denote:

(*a*) completed action, the result of which no longer remains;

Koppen **har varit lagad** en gång, men nu är den sönder igen.	The cup has been mended once but is now broken again.

(*b*) something that has been taking place for some time and is (was) still taking place.

Han **har varit förlovad** i sju år.	He has been engaged (to be married) for seven years.

233 The Passive of Verbs of Duration

(*a*) Present and Past: **s-forms** and periphrastic forms with **vara** denote proceeding action.

Han **fruktas** (*or:* **är fruktad**) av undersåtarna.	He is feared by his subjects.
Han **fruktades** (*or:* **var fruktad**) av undersåtarna.	He was feared by his subjects.

NOTE. — *Han* **blir** *fruktad* denotes beginning action in the future ('will be feared'). *Han* **blev** *fruktad* denotes beginning action in the past ('came to be feared').

---

[1] Not *varit!*

(*b*) Present Perfect and Past Perfect: **s-forms** and periphrastic forms with **vara** and **bliva** are interchangeable.

Passive Infinitive after Auxiliary Verbs

(*a*) **Skall** followed by **s-form** denotes Pre-arrangement, Wish or Demand.

Ett regemente **skall sändas** till Sydafrika.	One regiment *is to be sent* to South Africa.
Skorna **skall borstas** varje dag.	The shoes must be cleaned every day.

(*b*) **Skall** followed by a periphrastic form with **bli** denotes Promise, Assurance.

Han **skall bli** väl **mottagen.** He shall be well received.

(*c*) **Måste, bör, torde** followed by **s-form** denote Necessity, Wish, Demand.

Något måste **göras.**	Something must be done.
Flaskan bör **skakas** väl före begagnandet.	The bottle should be well shaken before use.
Anmälningar torde **sändas** till undertecknad.	Applications should be sent to the undersigned.

(*d*) **Bör, torde** followed by a periphrastic form with **bli** often denote Supposition or Probability.

Partiet **torde bli avsänt** inom en vecka.	The consignment *will probably be sent* within a week.
(Cf.: Partiet **torde avsändas** inom en vecka.	*Kindly send* the consignment within a week.)

USE OF THE PASSIVE VOICE

The Passive Voice has, on the whole, a more restricted use than in English. **235**

The Indirect Object of an active sentence cannot, as a rule, be made the Subject of a passive sentence. **236**

Man har sagt mig det.[1]	{ I have been told so.
Det har **sagts** mig.	{ It has been told me.
Man visade honom två tavlor.[2]	{ He was shown two pictures.
	{ Two pictures were shown him.

237 When there are two Direct Objects, one denoting a thing and the other a person, only the thing-object can be made the Subject of a passive sentence. Best is to avoid the passive construction altogether.

Jag fick lära mig en ny dans.	{ I was taught a new dance.
	{ A new dance was taught me.
Hon fick tre frågor.	{ She was asked three questions.
	{ Three questions were asked her.

238 A Verb followed by a Preposition cannot be turned into the Passive Voice, unless the Preposition (the adverbial element) forms part of a Separable Verb. (Cf. §§ 280—284.)

Man skrattade åt henne.	She was *laughed at*.
Man kommer säkert att ta hand om honom.	He is sure to be *taken care of*.
Det är inte att undra på.	It must not be wondered at.
Man har inte sett efter henne ordentligt.	She has not been properly looked after.
Ingen hade sovit i sängen.	The bed had not *been slept in*.

NOTE. — Separable verbs (see §§ 280—284) can be turned into the Passive Voice.

Mötet **sköts upp**.[3]	}
Mötet **uppsköts**.	} The meeting was postponed (put off).
Mötet **blev uppskjutet**.	}

Locket skruvades på.[3]	}
Locket påskruvades.	} The lid was screwed on.
Locket blev påskruvat.	}

---

[1] Not: *Jag har sagts det.*
[2] Not: *Han visades två tavlor.*
[3] The stress is on *upp, på.*

An English passive infinitive after the verbs 'to be', 'to remain', 'to **239**
leave', corresponds to an **active infinitive** in Swedish in expressions
like the following:

Vad är **att göra?**	What is *to be done?*
Det var **att vänta.**	It was *to be expected.*
Mycket återstår **att göra.**	Much remains *to be done.*
Utställningen lämnade åtskilligt övrigt **att önska.**	The exhibition left a great deal *to be desired.*
Följande historia **stod att läsa** i en Stockholmstidning.	The following story *was to be read* in a Stockholm newspaper.
Var kan man **få** (köpa) den här boken?	Where is this book *to be had?*

NOTE. — *Detta hus är* **till salu.**[1] 'This house is *to be sold.*'

The verbs 'to cause', 'to command', 'to order', 'to direct' followed **240**
by an object with a passive infinitive are rendered by **låta** with an
active infinitive.

Han **lät föra** in fången.	He ordered the prisoner to be brought in.
Ordföranden **lät uppläsa** protokollet över föregående sammanträde.	The chairman caused the minutes of the preceding meeting to be read.

NOTE. — After the verbs *se* 'to see' and *höra* 'to hear', a passive infinitive in Swedish corresponds to a past participle in English.

Vi såg träden **speglas** i vattnet.	We saw the trees *reflected* in the water.
Jag har hört **sägas,** att . . .	I have heard it *said* that . . .

Other Uses of the s-form

The verb-forms in **-s** are also used to express reciprocal action. **241**

De **möttes** på bron.	They met on the bridge.
Vi **hjälptes åt.**	We helped each other.
De **följdes åt** till stationen.	They went together to the station.

---

[1] Lit. 'on sale'.

Vi **ses** (or **träffas**) om fredag.	See you on Friday.
Vill du **slåss?**[1]	Will you fight?
De **skildes** som vänner.	They parted as friends.

242 Some s-forms acquire an active meaning

Akta dig, det **bränns**!	Take care, it will burn!
Han tycker om att **retas**.	He is fond of teasing.
Hunden **bits**.	The dog bites.
Narras inte!	Don't tell stories!
Knuffas inte!	Don't push!

Note the following impersonal expressions:

Det hördes (syntes), att han var arg [arj].	You could hear (see) that he was angry.
Det märks knappt.	It is hardly noticeable.
Hur **känns det** nu?	How are you feeling now?
Hur känns det att börja skolan igen?	What does it feel like beginning school again?
Kan jag hjälpa er? — Tack, **det behövs** [bəhœ′fs] inte.	Can I help you? — No thanks, there's no need to.

243 Deponent Verbs

Some Verbs have only **s**-forms. They are called Deponent Verbs. Deponent Verbs have **passive form but active meaning**.

Jag kan inte **andas**.	I cannot breathe.
Jag **hoppas,** att han kommer.	I hope he will come.
Jag **minns** inte, vad han sade.	I don't remember what he said.
Han **lyckades** rädda henne.	He managed to save her.
Hon **tycktes** sova.	She seemed to be asleep.

Other Deponent Verbs are: *envisas* 'be obstinate'; *brottas* 'wrestle'; *brås* (*på sin far*) 'take after (one's father)'; *kräkas* 'vomit'.

---

[1] Note the double **-s** with consequent shortening of preceding vowel: [sləs].

USE OF THE TENSES

Present   **244**

The Present is often used with Future meaning, especially in the case of Verbs of Motion and the verbs *bli* and *vara*, when the context indicates future time.

Han **kommer** i morgon.	He will come tomorrow.
Båten **går** nästa vecka.	The boat will leave next week.
Kommer ni tillbaka till klockan 5?	Will you be back by five?
Det **blir** mörkt om en liten stund.	It will be dark in a little while.
Jag **är** tillbaka om en halvtimme.	I shall be back in half an hour.
Tror ni, att han **hinner** med tåget?	Do you think he will catch the train?
Hur lång tid tror ni att det **tar?**	How long do you think it will take?
Väntar ni på mig, om jag kommer lite sent?	Will you be waiting for me if I am late?

Note the use of Present instead of Past in the following expressions:

När **är** ni född?	When were you born?
Jag **är** född den 14 juni 1947.	I was born on the 14th of June, 1947.

This only applies to living persons; in other cases the Past Passive *föddes* is used, e. g. *Shakespeare föddes 1564.*

Past   **245**

Swedish Past corresponds to English Present in impersonal constructions implying Feeling or Opinion.

Det **var** roligt, att du klarade dig i examen.	I am glad you passed in the examination.
Det **var** tråkigt, att du inte kan komma.	I am sorry you cannot come.
Det **var** synd, att du inte tänkte på det, medan han var här.	It's a pity you didn't think of it while he was here.

Det **var** länge, sedan jag såg dig.	It's a long time since I have seen you.
Det **var** väldigt snällt av er att komma och möta mig.	It's awfully good of you to meet me.

246 Present Perfect

Swedish Present Perfect sometimes corresponds to English Past, especially in sentences containing *någonsin* 'ever', and *aldrig* 'never'.

Var **har** ni **lärt** er engelska?	Where did you learn English?
Har ni **sovit** gott i natt?	Did you sleep well last night?
Har ni någonsin **sett** /på/ maken?	Did you ever see the like?
Det **har** jag aldrig **tänkt** på.	I never thought of that.
Har någon **varit** här, medan jag var ute?	Did anyone call while I was out?

Swedish Present Perfect refers to the future in cases like the following:

Jag **har** nog **slutat,** när du är färdig.	I am sure I shall have finished by the time you are ready.

247 Future

The usual way of expressing simple futurity in Swedish (without implying any Intention, Promise, Threat, etc.) is to use the phrase **kommer att** + the Infinitive of the Verb. Cf. § 250. This construction corresponds to English 'shall' (in the 1st person) and 'will' (in the 2nd and 3rd persons).

Jag **kommer** inte **att** sakna honom.	I shall not miss him.
Ni **kommer att** ångra er längre fram.	You will be sorry for it later on.
Det **kommer** inte **att** ske i vår livstid.	It will not happen in our lifetime.

NOTE. — In many cases the Present Tense is used with Future meaning. See § 244.

152

Future in the Past (Conditional)

The Future in the Past is used as in English. Sometimes the Past Subjunctive, or the Past Perfect Subjunctive, is used instead of the Future in the Past.

Jag **skulle** inte **göra** det, om jag vore som du.	I should not do it if I were you.
Ni **skulle göra** mig mycket förbunden genom att göra mig denna tjänst.	You would greatly oblige me by doing me this favour.
Jag **vore** (= skulle vara) tacksam för svar så snart som möjligt.	I should be thankful for a reply at your earliest convenience.
Det **hade** (= skulle ha) **varit** bättre, om vi hade stannat hemma.	It would have been better if we had stayed at home.
Hon **hade** gärna **velat** komma.	She would have liked to come.

NOTE. — In English **should** is used in the 1st person, **would** in the 2nd and 3rd persons. In Swedish **skulle** is used in all three persons.

Continuous Form

Swedish has no special Continuous (Progressive) Form such as English 'I am writing'. 'I write' (Simple Present) and 'I am writing' (Continuous Present) are both rendered by *jag skriver*. Where it is necessary to emphasize that the action is in progress, the phrase *hålla på*[1] *att* (lit. 'keep on to') may be used with a following infinitive.

Hur ofta skriver han?	How often does he write?
Han skriver en gång i veckan.	He writes once a week.
Vad **gör** du?	What *are* you *doing?*
Jag **skriver** brev.	I *am writing* a letter.
Regnar det?	*Is* it *raining?*
Det **regnar** varenda dag.	It rains every day.

---

[1] The stress is on *på*.

Jag **har läst** hela dagen.	I have been reading all day.
En ny kyrka **håller på att byggas.**	A new church is being built.
Vad **gjorde** du (or: Vad **höll du på med**), när jag kom in?	What were you doing when I came in?
Medan Olle **höll på** /**med**/ **att rigga** sin båt, gick Svante ut.	While Olle was rigging his boat, Svante went out.
Jag **skall gå** på teatern i kväll.	I am going to the theatre tonight.

USE OF THE AUXILIARY VERBS

Skall, skulle

250 **Skall** indicates Future, usually with the implied notion of Intention or Will, Promise or Threat. It is used in all three persons and so corresponds to English 'will', as well as 'shall'. If no Intention or Determination is implied, the Future may be expressed by **kommer att** instead of *skall*. Cf. §§ 244 and 247.

Jag **skall** (or: **kommer att**) se till, att han får tillbaka sina pengar.	I will (shall) see to it that he gets his money back.
Kungen **skall** (or: **kommer att**) öppna utställningen.	The King will (is going to) open the exhibition.
Han **skall** inte resa förrän i kväll. Han **reser** inte förrän i kväll. Han **kommer** inte **att** resa förrän i kväll.	He will not leave till tonight.
Jag **skall** nog hålla utkik själv, **skall** du få se.	I will be on the look-out myself, you shall see.
Var snäll och hälsa så mycket till dina föräldrar. — Tack, det **skall** jag göra.	Please remember me to your parents. — I will, thank you.

154

Skulle 'should', 'would', indicates Future in the past (and Conditional). Cf § 248.

Jag **skulle ha** hjälpt honom, om han hade bett mig.	I should have helped him if he had asked me.
Han **skulle** nog **ha** gjort det, om han hade kunnat.	I'm sure he would have done it if he had been able to.
Han lovade, att han inte **skulle** göra om det.	He promised that he would not repeat it.
Jag hade föresatt mig, att jag **skulle** göra det.	I had made up my mind that I would do it.
Jag **skulle** just gå ut, när du kom.	I was just going out when you came.

Skall (skulle) is also used to indicate an action which is dependent **251** on another person's Will, or on a Previous Arrangement. English equivalents: 'shall', 'is to'.

Skall jag stänga fönstret?	Shall I shut the window?
Ni **skall** få pengarna i morgon.	You shall have the money tomorrow.
Du **skall** icke dräpa.	Thou shalt not kill.
Vad **skall** pojken bli?	What *is* the boy /going/ *to* be?
Vad **ska** jag göra?	What *am* I /supposed/ *to* do?
Vi ska träffas vid stationen.	We *are to* meet at the station.
Kungen **skulle** vara närvarande.	The King *was to* be present.
De **skulle** komma under förmiddagens lopp.	They *were to* arrive during the morning.

NOTE. — *Skall (skulle)* is also used as an equivalent of 'ought to'.

Jag tycker, att han **ska** (= bör) gå till en läkare.	He should (ought to) see a doctor.
Ni **skulle** (= borde) inte ha talat om det för honom.	You should not (ought not to) have told him.

Skulle is used in Conditional Clauses where English has 'were to' **252** (or 'should').

Jag vet inte, vad som **skulle** hända, om han **skulle** försöka.	I do not know what would happen if he *were to* try.

155

253 *Skall* (*skulle*) corresponds to English 'should' after verbs and impersonal constructions expressing Feeling, Emotion or a personal Opinion.

Jag är ledsen (förvånad) över att han **skall** ljuga på det där sättet.	I am sorry (surprised) that he *should* tell such lies.
Det är helt naturligt, att ni **skall** tycka det.	It is quite natural that you *should* think so.
Det är synd, att han **skall** vara så dum.	It is a pity that he should be such a fool.
Hur /i all världen/ **skall** jag kunna veta det?	How /on earth/ should I know?

NOTE. — 'I shall', 'I will', 'I am going to', 'I am about to', 'I am on the point of', 'I am to', 'I am supposed to', all correspond to **jag skall** in Swedish.

Vill, ville

254 **Vill** (**ville**) always indicates volition (a Wish or a Desire) and is not used to indicate Future like English 'will'.

Vill ni följa med till stationen?	Will you go with me to the station?
Han frågade mig, om jag **ville** hjälpa honom.	He asked me if I would (was willing to) help him.
Tror ni, att han skulle **vilja** göra det?	Do you think he would *like to* do it?
Han **vill** bli ingenjör.	He *wants to* be an engineer.[1]
Vad **vill** ni? (Vad vill ni ha?)	What do you want?
Han får göra, som han **vill**.	He can do as he *likes* (pleases, chooses).
Jag **ville** inte besvära honom.	I did not want to trouble him.
Hon har aldrig **velat** göra det.	She has never *been willing* to do it.

---

[1] Cf. 'He will be an engineer' = *Han kommer att bli ingenjör.*

In English the verbs 'want' and 'like' are often followed by an **255** Object with the Infinitive. This construction cannot be used in Swedish after *vill*, but must be rendered by a Subordinate Clause beginning with **att**.

Han **ville** inte, **att** jag skulle veta det.	He *did not want me to know* it.
Jag skulle inte **vilja, att** han gjorde det.	I should not *like him to do* it.
Hon **ville, att** vi skulle hjälpa henne.	She *wanted us to help* her.

When English 'will' expresses Natural Propensity or Habit, it is **256** not translated by *vill* but by the Present of the main verb; 'would' is rendered by *brukade* ('used to'), *kunde* ('could'), or no auxiliary.

Detta tyg **krymper** icke.	This material will not shrink.
Pojkar **är** nu en gång pojkar.	Boys will be boys.
Han **kunde** sitta timtals och göra ingenting.	He would sit for hours doing nothing.
Sedan **brukade** han ta av sig rocken och börja. Han skickade hembiträdet efter för 50 öre spik, etc.	Then he would take off his coat and begin. He would send the girl out for sixpen'-orth of nails, etc.

The translation of 'may', 'might'   257

(*a*) 'May' is translated by **må** when it expresses a Wish or Concession.

Må (**Måtte**) du bli lycklig!	May you be happy.
Hur därmed än **må** förhålla sig.	However that may be.

(*b*) 'May' is translated by **kan** when it expresses a Polite Request.

Ni **kan** gärna göra det nu.	You may as well do it now.
Ni **kan** säga åt honom, att jag vill träffa honom.	You might tell him that I should like to see him.

157

(c) 'May', 'might' is translated by **skall, skulle** when it expresses an Intention.

Han gjorde det, för att de **skulle** få se, hur skicklig han var.	He did it that they might see how clever he was.

(d) 'May', 'might' is translated by **kan, kunde,** or with the help of the adverb **kanske** 'perhaps', when it expresses Possibility.

Det **kan** hända. (Kanske det.)	That may be /so/.
Det **kan** (kunde) vara sant.	It may (might) be true.
Det **kanske** inte är sant.	It may (might) not be true.
I en sådan situation **skulle** vad som helst **kunna** hända.	In such a situation anything might happen.
Han **kanske** gör det, om ni ber honom.	He may do it if you ask him.
Ni **kunde** göra er illa.	You might hurt yourself.

(e) 'May' is translated by **får** when it expresses Permission.

Får jag besvära om senapen?	May I trouble you for the mustard?
Får jag låna den här boken?	May I borrow this book? —
— Ja, det **får** ni.	Yes, you may.
Nej, det **får** ni inte.	No, you mayn't.

258 Måste

'Must' corresponds to **måste,** which form is used not only in the Present but also in the Past (= 'had to') and the Future (= 'will have to').

Han **måste** resa genast.	He must leave at once.
Han **måste** resa i går.	He *had to* leave yesterday.
Han **måste** resa nästa vecka.	He *will have to* leave next week.
Han har **måst** resa.	He has *been obliged to* leave.

NOTE. — 'Must not' is translated by **får inte,** when it expresses Prohibition.

Ni **får inte** göra det.	You must not do that.

158

Låta   **259**

Låta is used in two different senses: (*a*) 'to allow' and (*b*) 'to cause'.

(*a*) **Låt** mig hjälpa dig!   *Allow* me to help you.

Låt honom inte komma in!   Do not *let* him come in.

Mamma **låter** mig inte gå.   Mother does not allow me to go.

Han **lät** övertala sig.   He *suffered* (permitted, allowed) himself to be persuaded.

(*b*) Ordföranden **lät** uppläsa föregående mötes protokoll.   The chairman *caused* the minutes of the preceding meeting to be read.

Han **lät** dem arbeta som slavar.   He *made* them work like slaves.

Jag **lät** sekreteraren läsa upp brevet för mig.   I *asked* the secretary to read me out the letter.

Jag skall **låta** göra mig en ny kostym.   I am going to *have* a new suit made.

Jag **lät** skräddaren laga rocken.   I *got* the tailor to mend my coat.

Generalen **lät** skjuta desertören.   The general *ordered* the deserter to be shot.

Har jag **låtit** er vänta?   Have I *kept* you waiting?

NOTE. — *Låta* is also used to replace the imperative of the 1st person plural.

Låt oss gå på bio!   Let us go to the pictures!

Låtom[1] oss bedja!   Let us pray!

USE OF THE INFINITIVE, PARTICIPLES AND SUPINE

The Infinitive

The Infinitive is, as a rule, preceded by **att**.   **260**

Han kom mig **att skratta.**   He made me laugh.

Hellre än **att ge** vika beslöt han **att dö.**   Rather than yield he resolved to die.

---

[1] Old form (1st person plural) used in elevated style (poetry, Church usage, etc.).

261 When the Infinitive is used to express Intention, it is preceded by **för att** 'in order to', 'so as to', 'to'.

Han skrev ett brevkort **för att** tala om, att han var sjuk.	He wrote a post-card *to* say that he was ill.
Jag höll mig borta **för att inte** störa dem.	I kept away *so as not to* disturb them.
Han reste till Paris **för att** studera musik.	He went to Paris */in order/ to* (with a view to) study music.

NOTE. — When the Infinitive expresses what a substance or a thing is used for, it is preceded by *till att*.

Trä används **till att** göra papper av.	Wood is used to make (for making) paper.
Korgen används **till att** bära äpplen i.	The basket is used for carrying apples.

262 The Infinitive is used without **att**:

(*a*) after the Auxiliary Verbs (*skall, vill, kan, bör, får, måste*, etc.):

Det **borde** göras genast.	It ought to be done at once.
Vi **får** väl se.	We shall see.
Vad **vill** ni veta?	What do you want to know?

(*b*) after the following Verbs: *tänka* 'contemplate', 'be thinking'; *hoppas* 'hope'; *tyckas* 'seem'; *bruka* 'be in the habit of'; *behöva* 'need'; *önska* 'wish'; and a few others.

Jag **behövde** inte betala.	I did not have to pay.
När **tänker** ni resa?	When are you leaving?
Jag tänker inte göra om det.	I am not going to do it again.
Vad **ämnar** ni göra?	What do you intend to do?
Jag **hoppas** få träffa honom i morgon.	I hope to see him tomorrow.
Det **tycks** inte vara sant.	It does not seem to be true.
Han **försökte** hoppa över grinden.	He tried to jump over the gate.
Han **lärde sig** simma.	He learnt /how/ to swim.

160

Jag **lärde** honom simma.	I taught him /how/ to swim.
Han **brukade** ta en promenad före frukosten.	He used to take a walk before breakfast.
Skrivmaskinen **behöver** smörjas.	The typewriter requires oiling.
Han **lyckades** undkomma.	He managed to escape.
Han **bad** mig komma och hälsa på dem.	He asked me to come and see them.
De, som **önska** deltaga i tävlingen, ombedjas skriva sina namn på listan.	Those who want to take part in the match are asked to put their names on the list.
Det **började** regna.	It started to rain.

(c) In the constructions Object with the Infinitive and Subject with the Infinitive.

Jag hörde någon vissla.	I heard somebody whistle.
Någon hördes vissla.	Somebody was heard to whistle.
Rök sågs stiga upp (*or:* Man såg rök stiga upp).	Smoke was seen to be rising.
Jag anser honom inte vara fullt normal.	I don't consider him to be quite right in his head.
Han anses (påstås) vara mycket skicklig.	He is considered (said) to be very clever.

In the following cases an English Infinitive is rendered by **a full 263 Subordinate Clause** in Swedish:

(a) After the expression 'had better'.

Det är bäst, **att ni gör** det genast.	You had better do it at once.
Är det inte bäst, att du frågar din far först?	Hadn't you better ask your father first?

(b) When English has an Object with the Infinitive after verbs of volition such as 'want'; 'wish'; 'expect'. Cf. § 255.

	What do you want *him to do?*
Vad vill (önskar) ni, **att han skall göra?**	What would you like him to do? What do you wish (desire) him to do?
Jag väntade mig inte, **att hon skulle komma.**	I did not expect *her to turn up.*

(c) When English has an Object with the Infinitive after the preposition 'for'.

Jag väntade bara **på att han skulle gå.**	I was only waiting *for him to go.*
Jag längtar **efter att de skall komma.**	I am longing for them to come.
På den tiden var det inte vanligt, **att damer rökte** cigarretter.	At that time it was not customary for ladies to smoke cigarettes.

Det är mycket bättre, **att hon kommer** hit.	It is much better *for her to come* here.
Vägen var för smal (*or:* inte bred nog) för att två bilar skulle kunna mötas.	The road was too narrow (not wide enough) *for two cars to meet.*

Similarly:

Jag litar **på att hon hjälper** oss.	I rely *on her to help* us.

(d) When English has an Ordinal Number (or *the last, the next*) followed by an Infinitive. The English Infinitive is then rendered by a relative clause in Swedish.

Han var **den första** (tredje), **som försökte** det.	He was the first (third) to attempt it.

Similarly:

Kaptenen var **den siste, som lämnade** fartyget.	The captain was *the last* man *to leave* the ship.
Nästa sak, **som ramlade av,** var en lampa.	*The next* thing *to drop off* was a lamp.

162

(e) In expressions like the following:

Jag var dum, **som hjälpte** honom.	I was a fool *to help* him.
Ni vore dum, **om ni trodde** det.	You would be a fool *to believe* it.
Hur kunde han vara **så** dum, **att han trodde** det?	How could he be *so* foolish *as to believe* it?

(f) When English has an Infinitive after an Interrogative Pronoun or Adverb.

Jag vet inte, **vad jag skall göra** (vart jag skall gå).	I do not know what to do (where to go).
Kan ni säga mig, hur man skall öppna den här burken?	Could you tell me how to open this tin?
Han var osäker **på om han skulle resa** eller inte.	He was uncertain *whether to go* or not.
Jag skall säga till, **när ni skall** stanna.	I will tell you *when to stop*.

(g) When English has the construction 'be likely to', 'be sure to'.

Det är inte troligt, **att han kommer.**	He is not *likely to come*.
Det är säkert, **att han gör det.**	He is *sure to do it*.

Swedish Equivalents of the English Gerund

Swedish has no Gerund.[1] The English Gerund is, as a rule, rendered **264** by an Infinitive in Swedish.

Det tjänar ingenting till **att försöka.**	It is no use *trying*.
Han kunde inte låta bli **att skratta.**	He could not help *laughing*.

---

[1] The English Gerund is the **-ing** form of a verb when used as a noun, as in '*Seeing* is *believing*'; 'He is fond of *playing* football'.

Har ni slutat **röka?**	Have you given up *smoking?*
Har det slutat **regna?**	Has it stopped raining?
Uppskjut inte **att skriva!**	Don't put off writing!
Jag har härmed nöjet **sända** bifogade priskurant.	I have the pleasure *of sending* enclosed price-list.
Han håller på **att packa.**	He is busy *packing.*
Det är knappast värt **att nämnas.**	It is hardly worth *mentioning.*
Ingenting går upp emot **att segla.**	There is nothing like *sailing.*
Det är omöjligt **att veta,** vad som skulle kunna hända.	There is no knowing what might happen.
Jag brukar **stiga upp** tidigt.	I am in the habit *of rising* early.
Han reste dit **i hopp att träffa** sin far.	He went there *in the hope of meeting* his father.

NOTE. — After the verb *behöva* 'need', 'require', 'want', Swedish uses the passive infinitive as an equivalent of English Gerund.

Motorn behöver **lagas.**	The engine needs *repairing.*

265 When the English Gerund is preceded by a Possessive Adjective, a Genitive, or a Noun governed by a Preposition, it is usually translated by **a full clause** in Swedish.

Att jag är svag, ger er ingen rättighet att förolämpa mig.	*My being weak* gives you no right to insult me.
Jag hade ingenting emot **att hon var** där.	I did not mind *her being* there.
Vi kunde inte rå för, **att de förde** oväsen.	We could not help *their making* a noise.
Han tog bort knappen, **utan att pojken såg det.**	He removed the button *without the boy's seeing* it.
Hon gillade inte, att unga flickor gick sysslolösa.	She did not approve of young girls being idle.
Jag hoppas ni ursäktar, **att jag har låtit** er vänta.	I hope you will excuse *my having kept* you writing.

Kungen var belåten med stället, **emedan det låg** så avskilt.	The King was pleased with the place *owing to its being* so secluded.
Då han fick syn på Harris och mig, sprang han sin väg.	*On catching sight* of Harris and me, he ran away.

An English Gerund governed by a Preposition is usually rendered **266** by an Infinitive governed by a Preposition.

Han har förstört sina ögon **genom att läsa** för mycket.	He has spoilt his eyes *by reading* too much.
Han gjorde det **utan att tänka.**	He did it *without thinking.*
Lyckan består **i att göra** gott.	Happiness consists *in doing* good.
Hon reste utan uppehåll, **utom för att byta** hästar.	She travelled without a halt, *save for changing* horses.
Jag föredrar att resa med ångbåt **framför att resa** med tåg.	I prefer going by steamer *to travelling* by train.
Efter att ha ätit middag gick hon upp på sitt rum.	*After having* had her dinner, she went upstairs.

Subordinate Clauses are often governed by Prepositions in Swedish. **267**

Kan jag lita **på att ni kommer?**	Can I rely *on your coming?*
Han gick, **utan att jag visste** om det.	He went *without my knowing* it.
Olyckan berodde **på att de hade** följt hans råd.	The accident was due *to their having* followed his advice.
Är ni säker **på att** han inte är ute?	Are you sure he is not out?
Han påminde oss **om att** det var tid att gå hem.	He reminded us that it was time to go home.
Hon beklagade sig **över att** hon inte kunde få någon sittplats.	She complained that she could not get a seat.
Jag gratulerade honom med anledning **av att** han hade fått första pris i tävlingen.	I congratulated him *on the fact that* he had got the first prize in the competition.
Han var övertygad **om att** det skulle bli regn.	He was convinced it would rain.

268 Object with the Infinitive

Object with the Infinitive is often used after the verbs *se* 'see'; *höra* 'hear'; *befalla* 'command'; *låta* 'let'; *tillåta* 'allow'; *komma* 'make, cause'; *anse* 'consider'; and a few others.

Jag såg **honom komma.**	I saw him come.
Jag har hört henne sjunga.	I have heard her sing.
Han befallde dem att stanna.	He ordered them to stop.
Han lät (bad) mig fortsätta.	He allowed (asked) me to continue.
Det var det, som **kom mig att skratta.**	That is what made me laugh.
Jag anser honom vara kompetent.	I consider him to be competent.

(Passive Voice: *Han anses vara rik.* 'He is considered to be rich.')

NOTE. — An English Object with the Infinitive after verbs of volition must be translated by an **att**-clause.

Jag vill inte, **att hon skall komma.**	I do not want her to come.
Han skulle gärna vilja, **att vi stannade** kvar.	He would like us to stay on.

269

An English Object with the Infinitive after verbs like 'think', 'know', 'prove', must be translated by an **att**-clause.

Detta bevisade, **att han hade** orätt.	This proved *him to be* wrong.
Hon trodde, **att det var** ett skämt.	She took it to be a joke.
Jag vet, **att hon har gjort** det förr.	I have known *her to do* it before.

270

The verbs *tro* 'think'; *tycka* 'think'; *anse* 'consider'; *säga* 'say'; *påstå* 'contend', are often followed by a Reflexive Pronoun + Infinitive.

Han **trodde sig förstå,** vad hon menade. (Han trodde, att han förstod, vad . . .)	He thought he understood what she meant.
Hon påstod sig veta, vad det var. (Hon påstod, att hon visste, vad . . .)	She said she knew what it was.
Jag **tyckte mig höra** någon sjunga. (Jag tyckte, att jag hörde någon sjunga.)	I thought I heard somebody singing.
Han **ansåg sig inte kunna** göra det.	He did not think he could do it.

Swedish Equivalents of the English Present Participle

An English verb followed by a Present Participle (e. g. 'He sat **271** smoking') is often rendered in Swedish by (a) two coordinated verbs, or (b) a verb followed by an Infinitive, or (c) an Object with the Infinitive.

(a) Hon **stod och stirrade** på mig.	She *stood staring* at me.
De hade **stannat inne och läst** hela eftermiddagen.	They had *stopped in reading* all the afternoon.
Hon hade gått ut och handlat.	She had gone out shopping.
Han ville **gå och fiska.**	He wanted to *go fishing.*
Han brukar **sitta uppe och läsa** sent om nätterna.	He is in the habit of sitting up late reading at night.
(b) Han **fortsatte att tala.**	He went on talking.
Förlåt, att jag har **låtit er vänta.**	I am sorry I have kept you waiting.
(c) Jag hörde honom sjunga.	I heard him singing.
Jag kände något röra sig.	I felt something moving.
Vi såg två män släpas därifrån.	We saw two men being dragged away.

272 After the verb **komma** 'come', and sometimes after *bliva* 'remain', the Present Participle is used as in English.

Han **kom springande.**	He came running.
Han **blev liggande** i snödrivan.	He remained lying in the snow-drift.

273 Contracted Sentences (Participial Constructions) should be avoided in Swedish and substituted by full sentences.

Han skrev ett brevkort **och ta-lade om,** att han var sjuk.	He wrote a post-card *saying* that he was ill.
Då han såg, att det var omöjligt, gav han upp det.	*Seeing* that it was impossible, he gave it up.
Sedan han hållit detta tal, läm-nade han mötet.	*Having delivered* that speech, he left the meeting.
Eftersom Eder firma blivit oss re-kommenderad, skulle vi gärna vilja veta . . .	Your firm having been recom-mended to us, we should like to know . . .
När han lämnade stationen, hurrade folkmassan för honom.	*When leaving* the station he was cheered by the crowd.
Om Gud vill och vädret till-låter.	*God willing* and weather per-mitting.
En engelsman, **som reste** i Sve-rige, tog in på ett hotell.	An Englishman *travelling* in Swe-den put up at a hotel.

The Past Participle

274 In Swedish the Past Participle is not used after the auxiliary verb *ha/va/* to form compound tenses (Present Perfect and Past Perfect). For this purpose the Supine is used. See § 275.

The Past Participle is used as an Attributive or Predicative Adjective, mostly after the verbs **vara, bli/va/,** and in the periphrastic forms of the Passive Voice (see §§ 230—234). It is declined like an Adjective. See § 119—121.

168

Jag **blev presenterad** för honom på en bjudning.	I was introduced to him at a party.
Middagen **är serverad.**	Dinner is served.
De voro icke **väntade.**	They were not expected.
En **fallen** kung.	A fallen king.
Jag vill inte få min hatt och min kostym **förstörda** av regnet.	I do not want to have my hat and my suit spoilt by the rain.
Pengarna är **stulna.**	The money has been stolen.
Föreläsningen har **blivit uppskjuten.**	The lecture has been postponed.
Jag kan göra mig **förstådd.**	I can make myself understood.
Ett **brutet** löfte.	A broken promise.
Brevet **är skrivet.**	The letter has been written.
Fienderna **blevo slagna.**	The enemy were beaten.
Den **s. k.** (**så kallade**) studentexamen.	The so-called matriculation examination.
Det **övergivna** huset.	The abandoned house.

The Supine

The Supine is only used after the auxiliary verb *ha/va/* to form compound tenses (Present Perfect and Past Perfect). It is indeclinable. **275**

After the auxiliary verbs *vara* and *bli/va/* the Past Participle must be used instead of the Supine.

Compare the following examples:

SUPINE	PAST PATICIPLE
Jag **har skrivit** ett brev.	Brevet **är skrivet.**
'I have written a letter.'	'The letter has been written.'
Han borde **ha stängt** dörren.	Dörren borde **vara stängd.**
'He ought to have shut the door.'	'The door ought to be shut.'
Han **har kallat** många men **utvalt** få.	Många **äro kallade** men få **utvalda.**
'He has called many, but chosen few.'	'Many are called, but few chosen.'

SUPINE	PAST PARTICIPLE
Jag **har** inte **sett** till honom.	Han **blev sedd** av många.
'I have seen nothing of him.'	'He was seen by many.'
De **har lagat** sina maskiner.	De kunde inte **få** sina maskiner **lagade.**
'They have mended their machines.'	'They could not get their machines mended.'
Jag har inte **hört** honom tala.	Talaren kunde inte **göra sig hörd.**
'I have not heard him speak.'	'The speaker could not make himself heard.'
Han **har brutit** sina löften.	De **brutna** löftena.
'He has broken his promises.'	'The broken promises.'
Floderna **har frusit.**	De **frusna** floderna.
'The rivers have frozen.'	'The frozen rivers.'
Jag **har** aldrig **använt** kostymen.	Kostymen har aldrig **varit använd.**
'I have never worn the suit.'	'The suit has never been worn.'
De **har överraskat** oss.	Vi har **blivit överraskade.**
'They have taken us by surprise.'	'We have been taken by surprise.'
Vem **har sytt** din klänning?	Skorna **är handsydda.**
'Who has made your frock?'	'The shoes are hand-sewn.'

276 In Subordinate Clauses the Supine is sometimes used without an auxiliary verb (i. e. *har, hade*) to form Present Perfect and Past Perfect.

Som ni kanske redan **gissat** (= har gissat), hade han själv begått brottet.

As you may have guessed already, he had committed the crime himself.

Han svarade, innan han **blivit** (= hade blivit) tillfrågad.

He answered before he had been asked.

De hade kanske lyckats, om de försökt (= hade försökt) litet tidigare.

They would perhaps have succeeded if they had tried a little earlier.

170

Transitive and Intransitive Verbs

Many English verbs may be used either transitively (with an object, e. g. 'He sold his books') or intransitively (without an object, e. g. 'His books sold well'). In Swedish Transitive Verbs cannot, as a rule, be used intransitively or *vice versa*.

Han sålde sina böcker.	He sold his books.
Hans böcker **gick** bra.	His books sold well.
Hon öppnade dörren.	She opened the door.
Dörren **gick upp.**	The door opened.
Läste ni brevet?	Did you read the letter?
Brevet **lyder** som följer.	The letter reads as follows.
Vi fyllde korgen med äpplen.	We filled the basket with apples.
Hennes ögon **fylldes** av tårar.	Her eyes filled with tears.
Man **bränner** ved i kakelugnarna.	They burn wood in the stoves.
Trä **brinner.**	Wood burns.

Some verbs that are transitive in English are intransitive in Swed- **278** ish, e. g.: *gå in i ett rum* 'enter a room'; *kämpa emot någon* 'fight somebody'; *gå in vid armén* 'join the army'; *gå förbi någon* 'pass somebody'; *inverka på en person* 'influence a person'; etc.

Reflexive Verbs

Some verbs that are not reflexive in English are reflexive in Swed- **279** ish, e. g.: *visa sig* 'appear'; 'prove', 'turn out'; *närma sig* 'approach'; *förändra sig* 'change'; *lära sig* 'learn'; *gifta sig /med/* 'marry'; *missta/ga/ sig* 'be mistaken'; etc.

De har inte **förändrat sig** mycket.	They have not changed much.
Har du **ändrat dig?**	Have you changed your mind?
Hon **beklagade sig** över att hon inte kunde sova.	She complained that she could not sleep.
Ni kan **föreställa er** vår förvåning.	You may imagine our surprise.
Han **lärde sig** franska på tre månader.	He learnt French in three months.

Hon **gifte sig med** en präst.	She married a clergyman.
Jag **kände mig** inte riktigt bra.	I did not feel quite well.
De **rörde sig** inte.	They did not move.
En främling, som **visade sig** vara kungen av Spanien.	A stranger, who proved (turned out) to be the King of Spain.
Jag kan inte **åta/ga/ mig** att göra det.	I cannot undertake to do it.
Vi **närmade oss** stranden.	We were approaching the shore.
Trupperna **drog sig** tillbaka.	The troops retired.
Han kom, medan jag höll på att **klä mig** till middagen.	He came while I was dressing for dinner.
Jag hade inte **rakat mig.**	I had not shaved.
Lägg er på soffan!	Lie down on the couch!
Sätt dig på den där stolen!	Sit down on that chair!
Vi **väntade oss** inte att träffa honom där.	We did not expect to find him there.
Om jag inte **misstar mig.**	If I am not mistaken.
Skynda er!	Hurry up!

Separable and Inseparable Verbs

280 Compound Verbs are formed by combining a simple verb with a Prefix, a Noun, an Adjective, an Adverb or a Preposition. They are divided into Separable and Inseparable Verbs.

281 Verbs formed with one of the following Prefixes are **inseparable.**

EXAMPLES:

anklaga[1]	accuse	**miss**ta/ga/ sig	be mistaken
betala	pay	**sam**arbeta	cooperate
bispringa	succour	**um**gås	associate
erkänna	confess	**und**vika	avoid
förklara	explain	**van**ställa	disfigure
härstamma	be descended	**åta**/ga/ sig	undertake

NOTE. — (a) Most of these verbs are borrowed from the German.

---

[1] A few verbs formed with **an-** are separable, e. g. *angå*. Cf. § 283.

172

NOTE. — (*b*) The prefixes **be-** and **för-** are unstressed, and verbs formed with these prefixes have Tone I^1, e. g. *befalla* 'command'; *förstå* 'understand'.

Verbs formed with any of the other prefixes in the above list are pronounced with Tone II (with principal stress on the prefix), e. g. *anfalla* 'attack'; *bispringa* 'succour'.

NOTE. — (*c*) Compound Verbs having a Noun or Adjective as first element are inseparable, e. g. *rådfråga* 'consult'; *godkänna* 'approve'. They have Tone II with principal stress on the first element.

Compound Verbs formed with an Adverb or Preposition, excluding **282** the prefixes mentioned in § 281, have, as a rule, one **separable** and one **inseparable** form, e. g.:

känna igen	*or* igenkänna	recognize
stryka under	*or* understryka	underline
följa med	*or* medfölja	accompany
gå till	*or* tillgå	come about, happen
slita sönder	*or* sönderslita	tear up
tala om	*or* omtala	mention

In colloquial speech the separable forms are preferred.

NOTE. — (*a*) In the separable forms the stress is, as a rule, on the Adverb or the Preposition. The Verb itself is unstressed, e. g. [çɛna ijɛ′n].

NOTE. — (*b*) The inseparable forms have Tone II and principal stress on the prefix, e. g. [ijɛ′nçɛˋna].

NOTE. — (*c*) Many verbs compounded with an Adverb or a Preposition only occur as inseparable verbs, e. g. *invända* 'object'; *framhärda* 'persist'; *övergiva* 'abandon'; *förebygga* 'prevent'; *inverka* /*på*/ 'influence'.

---

^{1} EXCEPTION: *bearbeta* 'work upon', 'work up', which has stress on the **be-** and Tone II: [be:′arbe:ˋta].

283 In some Compound Verbs the inseparable form has a different meaning from the separable form. Compare:

Vad **står på?**	Han **påstår** det.
'What is up?'	'He says so.'
Han **bröt av** käppen.	Han **avbröt** samtalet.
'He broke the stick.'	'He broke off the conversation.'
Det **går** inte **för sig.**	Vad **försiggår** här?
'It will not do.'	'What is happening here?'
Hur **står** det **till?**	Han **tillstår** sitt fel.
'How are you?'	'He admits his fault.'
Det **går an.**	Det **angår** oss inte.
'It will do.'	'It does not concern us.'
Fartyget **gick under.**	Hon **undergick** en stor förändring.
'The ship went down.'	'She underwent a great change.'

NOTE. — As a rule, the inseparable forms are used in a figurative sense.

284 The Present Participle and Past Participle of Compound Verbs of all categories are **inseparable.** Compare:

Passagerarna **steg av** tåget.	De **avstigande** passagerarna.
'The passengers left the train.'	'The passengers leaving the train.'
Tio ombud **tog del** i förhandlingarna.	De i förhandlingarna **deltagande** ombuden.
'Ten delegates took part in the negotiations.'	'The delegates taking part in the negotiations.'
Jag **körde ut** honom.	Han blev **utkörd.**
'I turned him out.'	'He was turned out.'
De **valde om** honom.	Han har blivit **omvald.**
'They re-elected him.'	'He has been re-elected.'
Tala inte **om** det!	Det **omtalade** dokumentet.
'Don't mention it!'	'The above-mentioned document.'

174

Vilka ord har ni **strukit över**?	Inga ord är **överstrukna.**
'Which words have you crossed out?'	'No words are (have been) crossed out.'
De **kände** genast **igen** mig.	De blev genast **igenkända.**
'They recognized me at once.'	'They were recognized at once.'
Vem har **slagit sönder** fönstret?	Det **sönderslagna** fönstret.
'Who broke the window?'	'The broken window.'

Adverbs

A great many Adverbs are formed from Adjectives by adding **-t**   **285** (the Adverb thus being identical with the neuter form of the corresponding Adjective). Compare:

En vacker villa.	A beautiful villa.
Villan var mycket vacker.	The villa was very beautiful.
Villan var **vackert** belägen.	The villa was beautifully situated.
Hon sjunger **vackert.**	She sings beautifully.
De voro mycket lyckliga.	They were very happy.
De levde lyckligt tillsammans.	They lived happily together.
Trogna vänner.	Faithful friends.
De följde honom **troget.**	They accompanied him faithfully.

NOTE. — (a) The -t ending of a Swedish adverb corresponds to the **-ly** ending of an English adverb: *vackert* — beautifully.

NOTE. — (b) The word *bra* is used both as an adjective (inflexible, see §§ 90 and 97) and as an adverb (without the -t ending), e. g. *en bra lärare* 'a good teacher'; *han talar bra* 'he speaks well'.

Present Participles may be used as Adverbs. They take no -t ending.   **286**

Hon är **förtjusande** söt.	She is awfully (*lit.* charmingly) pretty.
Det är **rasande** svårt.	It is frightfully difficult.

NOTE. — The neuter form of the Past Participle may be used as an adverb, e. g. *Han arbetade* **hängivet** *för fredens sak* 'He worked devotedly in the cause of peace'.

287 Many Adverbs correspond to Pronouns and may be divided into Demonstrative, Relative, Interrogative and Indefinite Adverbs.

(*a*) **Demonstrative adverbs**

här, hit	here	härifrån	from here
där, dit	there	därifrån	from there
överallt	everywhere	härav	from this
nu	now	därav	from that
då, sedan	then	häruti, häri	in this
så	so	däruti, däri	in that
därför	therefore, therefor	härom	of this
härmed	herewith, hereby	därom	of that
härigenom	by this	häremot	against this
därmed	with that	däremot	on the other hand
därigenom	by that		

(*b*) **Relative adverbs**

där, dit	where	varifrån	from where
vari	wherein, in which	varom	of which
varav	whereof, of which	varuti	in which

NOTE. — English 'where' as a Relative Adverb is translated by **där** and **dit**. (Cf. § 292.)

Stanna **där** du är!	Stay *where* you are!
Han reste till Stockholm, **dit** hans familj hade rest före honom.	He went to Stockholm, *where* his family had gone before him.

(*c*) **Interrogative adverbs**

var?	where?	när?	when?
vart?	where to?	hur/u/?	how?

176

varifrån? where from? varför? why?
varmed? wherewith? vartill? whereto?

and others composed of *var* and a Preposition.

(d) **Indefinite adverbs**

någonstädes	somewhere	hur som helst	anyhow
ingenstädes	nowhere	var som helst	anywhere
annorlunda	otherwise	vart som helst	to anywhere
när som helst	at any time		

(e) **Indefinite relative adverbs**

Kom **när** du vill!   Come *whenever* you like!
Var han är, är han i vägen.   *Wherever* he is, he is in the way.

The Indefinite Relative Adverbs are often emphasized by the addition of **än** or **helst.**

Hur det **än** går.   However it goes.
Vare härmed **hur som helst.**   Be this as it may.
Hur rik han **än** är.   However rich he is (he may be).
Vart/helst/ han vände sig,   Whichever way he turned, he
    såg han bara bryggor.   saw nothing but jetties.

The adverb **ja** 'yes', answers to a question expressed affirmatively; **288** **jo** 'yes', answers to a question expressed negatively, or contradicts a negative statement.

Vill ni ha ett äpple? — **Ja** tack.   Will you have an apple? — Yes,
     please.
Vill ni **inte** ha ett äpple? — **Jo**   Won't you have an apple? —
    tack.   Yes, please.
Han kommer nog **inte.** — **Jo,**   I am afraid he will not come. —
    det gör han säkert.   Yes, I am sure he will.

Jo and **ja** also correspond to English 'oh', 'why', 'well', in ex- **289** planatory expressions like the following:

Vad är det där? — **Jo,** det är en skrivmaskin.	What is that? — *Oh,* it is a typewriter.
Vem tror ni, att det var? **Jo,** det var Alice!	Who do you think it was? *Why,* it was Alice!
Vad är orsaken? — **Ja,** det är svårt att säga.	What is the reason? — *Well,* it's difficult to tell.

COMPARISON OF ADVERBS

290 Adverbs derived from Adjectives form their degrees of comparison in the same way as the Adjectives. Cf. §§ 92—99.|

tidigt	early	tidigare	tidigast
omsorgsfullt	carefully	omsorgsfullare	omsorgsfullast
lågt	lowly	lägre	lägst
högt[1]	high/ly/	högre[1]	högst[2]

291 A few Adverbs not derived from Adjectives also have degrees of comparison:

ofta	often	oftare	oftast		
fort	quickly	fortare	fortast		
väl, bra	well	bättre	bäst		
illa	badly	värre	värst		
gärna	willingly	hellre	rather	helst	preferably
nära	near	närmare	närmast		
				näst	next

REMARKS ON CERTAIN ADVERBS

292 Some Adverbs of Place have two forms, one used with a Verb of Motion (indicating **Direction**) and the other used with a Verb indicating **Rest**. Compare the following examples:

Han gick **in.**	He went in.
Han är **inne.**	He is in.
Han gick **ut.**	He went out.
Han är **ute.**	He is out.

---

[1] *Tala högt* 'speak aloud'. *Tala högre!* 'Speak louder'!

[2] *Det var högst egendomligt!* 'That is very extraordinary.'

Min far reste **bort** i går, och han har inte kommit **hem** än.	My father went away yesterday, and he has not come home yet.
Han har varit **borta** sedan i går och är inte **hemma** än.	He has been away since yesterday and is not home yet.
Vart har han rest?	Where is he gone to?
Var är han?	Where is he?
Kom **hit**!	Come here!
Jag är **här**.	I am here.
Han har gått **dit**.	He has gone there.
Han är **där** nu.	He is there now.
Stanna **där** du är!	Stay where you are!
Han gick inte **dit** han skulle.	He did not go where he ought to have gone.
Hur dags [daks] stiger ni **upp**?	What time do you get up?
Jag är alltid **uppe** före sju.	I am always up by seven.
Hon gick **upp** (på sitt rum).	She went upstairs.
Hon är där **uppe** (däruppe).	She is up there (upstairs).
Hon gick **ner**.	She went down (downstairs).
Hon är där **nere**.	She is down there (downstairs).
När kommer vi **fram**?	What time do we get there?
Vi är redan **framme**.	We are there already.

Some Swedish Adverbs have no exact equivalents in English, e. g.: **293**
nog, väl, eller hur, gärna, hellre, helst, ju, ju . . . desto, visserligen, nämligen, kvar, tyvärr.

The following examples show their use:

Han är **nog** sjuk.	He is probably ill.
Det blir **nog** regn i morgon.	I am afraid it will rain tomorrow.
Han vet **nog** inte av det ännu.	I don't think he knows it yet.
Ni klarar det **nog**.	You will manage all right.
Ni har **väl**[1] hört, att han har rest?	I suppose you have heard that he has left?

---

[1] When used in this sense the word *väl* is unstressed.

Han kunde **väl** inte hjälpa det, kan jag tro.	I suppose he couldn't help it.
Ni går **väl** med på teatern i kväll, **eller hur?**	You will be going with us to the theatre tonight, *won't you?*
Jag skall **gärna** hjälpa honom.	I'll gladly (willingly) help him. (I shall be glad to help him.)
Jag skulle **gärna vilja** veta.	I should *like to* know.
Gärna för mig.	I have no objection. (I don't mind.)
Jag stannar **lika gärna** hemma.	I'd *just as soon* stay at home.
Jag stannar **helst** (**hellre**) hemma.	I prefer to (would rather) stay at home.
Ju förr **desto** (*or:* **dess**) bättre.	*The* sooner *the* better.
Jag kan **ju** inte veta, vad han tänker på.	I can't tell what he is thinking of, *can I?*
Jag har **ju** aldrig sett honom förr.	I have never seen him before, *you know.*
Han är **visserligen** äldre än jag, men han ser mycket yngre ut.	He is older than me, *it is true,* but he looks very much younger.
Jag känner honom mycket väl. Vi var **nämligen** skolkamrater.	I know him very well. We were at school together, *you see.*
Snön ligger **kvar** hela sommaren.	The snow remains all the summer.
Är det något **kvar** i flaskan?	Is there anything *left* in the bottle?
Jag kan **tyvärr** inte komma.	*I am sorry* I cannot come.
Hur **långt** gick ni?	How far did you go?
Hur **länge** stannade ni?	How long did you stay?
Så här gör man.	This is the way it is done.
Tycker ni om bananer? — Nej, **inte så värst**. — Det gör **inte** jag **heller**.	Do you like bananas? — No, not very much. — *Nor* do I.
Det **allra** bästa.	The best *of all.*

The word **förstås,** which is really the passive form of the verb
förstå 'understand', is used as an Adverb in the sense of 'of course'.
It is then pronounced [fəʂtɔ´s].

Det visste han **förstås** inte.　　　He didn't know it, of course.

Redan. Först　　　　　　　　　　　　　　　　　295

The adverb *redan* 'already' is also used in the sense of 'as early as', 'even'.

Redan på 1500-talet.　　　　　*As early as* the 16th century.
Redan nästa dag.　　　　　　　On *the very* next day.
Redan som barn skrev han　　*Even* as a child he wrote novels.
romaner.

The adverb *först* 'first' is also used in the sense of 'not until', 'only'.

Först[1] då fick jag höra talas om　*Not until* then did I hear about it.
det.
Jag kom **först**[1] i morse.　　　　I arrived *only* this morning.

Då. Sedan　　　　　　　　　　　　　　　　　296

English 'then' is translated by **då** when it means 'at that moment',
or 'in that case'.

English 'then' is translated by **sedan** when it means 'after that',
'subsequently', i. e. in a sequence of actions.

Just **då** fick han syn på en tjur. **Då** började han springa.	Just then he caught sight of a bull. Then he started to run.
En dag skulle geten gå ut i skogen efter mat. **Då** kallade hon till sig alla killingarna och sade: »Om vargen kommer, så öppna inte, för **då** äter han upp er.» — »Vi ska nog akta oss», svarade killingarna. — **Då** bräkte geten och gick ut i skogen.	One day the goat was going out into the wood to get some food. Then she called all the kids and said, "If the wolf comes, do not open the door, for then he will eat you." — "We will take care," answered the kids. — Then the goat bleated and went out into the wood.

---

[1] When used in this sense the word *först* is unstressed.

Vargen gick först till en handels-
man och köpte ett stycke
krita... **Sedan** gick han till en
bagare och bad honom stryka
lite deg på tassen... **Sedan**
gick han till en mjölnare och
bad honom strö lite mjöl på
tassen. **Sedan** gick han till-
baka och knackade på dörren.

Vad ska vi göra, om det regnar? — **Då** stannar vi hemma.
Han drack en kopp te och gick
sedan och lade sig.
Och **sedan då**?

The wolf first went to a shop-
keeper and bought a piece of
chalk... Then he went to a
baker and asked him to put
some dough on his paw...
Then he went to a miller and
asked him to sprinkle some
flour on his paw. Then he
went back and knocked at the
door.

What shall we do if it rains? —
Then we will stop at home.
He drank a cup of tea and then
went to bed.
And then?

NOTE. — *Sedan* and *då* may also be temporal Conjunctions. See §§ 303
and 304.

Conjunctions

297 The principal Conjunctions are:

och	and	förrän, innan	before
samt	and	/lika/ ... som	/as/ ... as
både ... och	both ... and	liksom ... /så/	as ... /so/
såväl ... som	as well ... as	/icke så/ ... som	/not so/ ... as
antingen...	either ...	som om	as if, as though
eller	or	än	than
varken ... eller	neither ... nor	så att	that, so that
icke endast ...	not only ...	för att	so that
utan /också/	but /also/	på det att[1]	/in order/ that
icke blott ...	not only ...		
utan även	but also		

---

[1] Only in the written language.

dels ... dels	partly ... partly	på det att icke[1]	lest, so that —
än ... än	now ... now		not
eller	or	därför att⎫ emedan[1]⎭	because
men	but	eftersom⎫	
utan	but	enär[1]⎬ då⎭	as, since
ty[1] (coll. för)	for	om; så framt;	if
att	that	såvida	
då, när	when	om (såvida) ...	unless
närhelst	whenever	icke	
medan,	while	om ... bara⎫	as long as
under det att		för så vitt /som/⎭	
sedan	after	förutsatt att	provided
allt sedan	since	ehuru[1],	/al/though
tills; till dess	until	fastän (coll. fast)	
/just/ som,	/just/ as	om än, oaktat[1]	even though
i det att		vare sig ...	whether ...
så länge som	as long as	eller	or
så snart som	as soon as	hur ... än	however
som; liksom;	as	om, huruvida	if, whether
allt efter som			

EXAMPLES ILLUSTRATING THE USE OF CERTAIN
CONJUNCTIONS

Men : utan   298

Han är fattig **men** hederlig.   He is poor but honest.
Han har inget hem, **utan** måste   He has no home but is obliged
  bo än hos den ene, än hos den   to stay now with one now with
  andre av sina släktingar.   another of his relatives.
Men is used after an affirmative; **utan** is used after a negative phrase
or clause when a contrast is implied.

---

[1] Only in the written language.

299 För: ty

»Du kan få alla tre yxorna, **för**   "You can have all three axes, for
(*or:* ty) du är en bra karl»,   you are a good fellow," said
sade tomten.   the elf.

For is colloquial; *ty* is only used in the written language.

300 Nämligen

Min bror ligger i dag. Han är   My brother is in bed today, be-
nämligen inte riktigt bra.   cause he is not quite well.

Nämligen, which is really an Adverb[1], often corresponds to 'for' or
'because' in English.

301 Så

Vänta lite, **så** får ni se!   Wait a little, *and* you will see!
Om ni går dit i morgon, **så** träf-   If you go there tomorrow, you
far ni honom.   will meet him.

Så corresponds to English 'and' after a clause expressing Command,
Promise, etc.

Så, without any corresponding Conjunction in English, often in-
troduces a Principal Clause following a Subordinate Clause.
In both cases *så* may be left out.

302 The translation of 'as'

Hon är **lika** snäll **som** begåvad.   She is *as* good *as* she is clever.
Kom **så snart** /som/ ni kan!   Come *as* soon *as* you can!
Vi gick **ända till** slottet.   We walked *as far as* the castle.
Silver är **inte så** dyrt **som** guld.   Silver is *not so* valuable *as* gold.
Han levde och dog **som** prote-   He lived and died a Protestant.
   stant.

---

[1] Cf. Hon talar tre främmande språk, *nämligen* franska, tyska och italienska 'She
speaks three foreign languages, *viz.* French, German and Italian'.

Som (**Medan**; **Bäst**) jag stod där, såg jag en man hoppa i floden.

As I stood there, I saw a man jump into the river.

/**Efter**/**som** jag inte hade några pengar, /så/ kunde jag inte köpa båten.

As I had no money, I could not buy the boat.

Då 303

Distinguish between (a) the Adverb *då* 'then', and (b) the Conjunction *då* 'when', 'as'. After the Adverb the word-order is **inverted,** but not after the Conjunction.

(a) Då **gör det** ingenting.   Then it doesn't matter.
Då **gick de** hem.   *Then* they went home.

(b) Då **de gick** hem, hände det en olycka.   *When* they went home, an accident happened.
Då **jag inte hade** några pengar, kunde jag inte resa.   As I had no money, I could not go.

Compare the following sentences:

Då **öppnade räven** munnen, och tuppen flög upp i ett träd.   *Then* the fox opened his mouth, and the cock flew up into a tree.
Då **räven öppnade** munnen, flög tuppen upp i ett träd.   *When* the fox opened his mouth, the cock flew up into a tree.

Sedan 304

Sedan may be (a) an Adverb, (b) a Conjunction or (c) a Preposition.

(a) Sedan **gick han** till en mjölnare.   *Then* he went to a miller.

(b) Sedan **han hade gått,** var de inte rädda längre.   *After* he had gone, they were not afraid any longer.
Sedan **han for,** har vi inte hört något av honom.   *Since* he went away, we have had no news of him.

(c) Jag har känt honom **sedan** I have known him *since* that
    den tiden.   time.
  Han reste till Amerika **för** He left for America three years
    tre år **sedan.**   *ago.*

NOTE. — For the distinction between *då* and *sedan* as temporal Adverbs, see § 296.

305 När: då

Jag gick ut, **när** (*or:* **då**) han I went out when he came in.
  kom in.

När and **då** are interchangeable as temporal Conjunctions; but **när** is more common in the spoken language.

306 Att

The Conjunction *att* should not be omitted in Swedish.

Hur visste han, **att** jag var här? How did he know /that/ I was here?

Jag sade åt honom, **att** han var I told him he was a fool.
  dum.

Han svor **på att** han aldrig hade He swore he had never seen her
  sett henne förut.   before.

307 The translation of 'that'

'That' may be (*a*) a Demonstrative Pronoun, (*b*) a Relative Pronoun, or (*c*) a Conjunction.

(*a*) Vem är **den där** karl/e/n? Who is *that* fellow?
    Just **den** natten.   } *That* very night.
    Redan **samma** kväll.

(*b*) Var det ni, **som** knackade? Was it you *that* knocked?

(*c*) Jag sade honom, **att** han I told him *that* he had got to do
    måste göra det.   it.

186

Nu då han har rest, kan man inte göra något åt saken.

Now that he is gone, nothing can be done in the matter.

Det var i det ögonblick, då de engelska katolikernas sista förhoppningar skingrats, **som** Maria Stuart landsteg i Leith.

It was at the moment when the last hopes of the English Catholics had been shattered, *that* Mary Stuart landed at Leith.

Prepositions

The principal Prepositions are:

angående		innan	before
beträffande	concerning	inom	within
rörande		med	with
av	of, by	medelst	by means of
bakom	behind	omkring; kring	about
efter	after	på; ovanpå	on, on top of
enligt	according	sedan	since
emot; mot	towards, against	till	to, till
emellan; mellan	between	trots	in spite of
framför; före	before	under	under, below,
från; ifrån	from		during
för ... sedan	ago	utan	without
för ... skull	for ... sake	uti (= i)	in
hos	with, at	utom	except
i	in	vid; bredvid	beside
ibland, bland	among	åt	to
igenom; genom	through	över	over, above

In certain fixed expressions some prepositions are placed after the word they govern, e. g. *oss emellan* 'between ourselves'; *hela natten igenom* 'all night'; *jorden runt* 'round the world'. **309**

310 When the word governed by the preposition is placed at the beginning of the sentence, the preposition should be placed at the end.

Kor är jag inte rädd **för.**   I am not afraid of cows.

This is always the case after the Relative Pronoun **som.**

Papperet, **som** jag skriver **på**   The paper on which I am
(*or:* **på vilket** jag skriver).   writing.

311 The preposition is very often placed at the end of à sentence beginning with an Interrogative Pronoun.

Vad tänker ni **på?**   What are you thinking of?
Vad gråter du **för?** (Varför grå-   What are you crying for?
ter du?)

312 The prepositions **till** and **i** are used with the genitive of the Noun in a few common phrases, e. g.:

till lands	by land	i onsdags	last Wednes-
till sjöss	to sea		day
till bords	at table	i julas	last Christmas
till fots	on foot	i vintras	last winter
till sängs	to bed	i somras	last summer

313 EXAMPLES OF THE TRANSLATION OF CERTAIN ENGLISH PREPOSITIONS

About

Frågade han er **om** det?   Did he ask you about it?
Har ni några pengar **på** er?   Have you any money about you?
Omkring (ungefär) kl. 3.   At about 3 o'clock.
Tänk på vad du gör!   Mind what you are about!
Det finns intet högmod **hos**   There is no pride about him.
    honom.

188

Ago

För fem år **sedan**[1] reste han hemifrån.

Five years ago he left home.

At

Titta inte **på** mig!	Don't look at me.
Månen skiner **om** natten.	The moon shines at night.
Han såg ut **genom** fönstret.	He looked out at the window.
Han stod **vid** fönstret.	He was standing at the window.
Han är **i** skolan.	He is at school.
Han bor i Uppsala.	He lives at Uppsala.
Hon bor **hos** sin moster.[2]	She is staying at her aunt's.
Jag såg dig **på** teatern i går.	I saw you at the theatre yesterday.
Han bor **på** Carlton.	He is staying at the Carlton.
Ångaren har anlänt **till** Stockholm.	The steamer has arrived at Stockholm.
Vid vilken tid väntar ni honom.	At what time do you expect him?
Han brukar komma **vid** julen.	He generally comes at Christmas.
På den tiden.	At that time.
Den såldes **till** högt pris.	It was sold at a high price.
Skratta inte **åt** henne!	Don't laugh at her.
I full fart.	At full speed.
Just **i** det ögonblicket.	At that very moment.
Jag har inte sett honom **alls.**	I have not seen him *at all.*

By

Kom och sitt **vid** (framför) brasan!	Come and sit by the fire!
Reste ni **över** Göteborg?	Did you go by Gothenburg?
Ni kommer dit **vid** den här tiden i övermorgon.	You will be there by this time the day after tomorrow.
Jag kommer tillbaka **till** klockan 8.	I shall be back by 8 o'clock.

---

[1] Often pronounced [sɛn].
[2] Lit. 'with her aunt'.

189

Han hatades **av** folket.	He was hated by the people.
Reser ni **med** tåg eller båt?	Are you going by train or by steamer?
Jag åker /med/ spårvagn.	I am going by tram.
Man kan inte gå **efter** regler i detta fall.	You cannot go by rules in this case.
Han får betalt **per** timme.	He is paid by the hour.
Han är ingenjör **till** yrket.	He is an engineer by profession.
Han gick **för** sig själv.	He went by himself.
Lär er det här stycket **utantill!**	Learn this paragraph *by heart*.

For

Han reste **till** Amerika i förra veckan.	He left for America last week.
Jag har inte sett honom **på** mycket länge.	I have not seen him for ever so long.
Han kommer att vara borta /**på**/ ett par dagar.	He will be away for a day or two.
Han har inte varit hemma /**under**/ de sista dagarna.	He has not been at home *for* the last few days.
Av brist **på** pengar.	For want of money.
Det var **ingen annan råd än** att ge efter.	There was *nothing for it but* to give in.
Vad får vi **till** middag?	What are you going to give us for dinner?
Hon grät **av** glädje.	She wept for joy.
Jag skulle ha drunknat, om inte han hade hjälpt mig.	I should have been drowned *but for him*.
Han längtade **efter** att dagen skulle gry.	He longed *for day to break*.
Väntar hon **på** mig?	Is she waiting for me?

In

Jag mötte honom **på** gatan.	I met him in the street.
Visby ligger **på** Gotland.	Visby is situated in the island of Gotland.

De anlände **till** London i går.	They arrived in London yesterday.
Vi bor **på** landet om somrarna.	We live in the country in summer.
På morgonen; **på** eftermiddagen.	In the morning; in the afternoon.
Under drottning Viktorias regering.	In the reign of Queen Victoria.
Jag kommer tillbaka **om** en fjorton dar.	I shall be back in about a fortnight.
På himlen.	In the sky.
Hon är född 1945.	She was born *in* 1945.
Till svar å Eder skrivelse ber jag få meddela . . .	In reply to your letter I beg to say . . .
Vad heter det **på** svenska?	What is that in Swedish?

Into

Han ramlade **i** sjön.	He fell into the water.
Han gick **in i** en affär.	He went into a shop.
Översätt det här **till** svenska!	Translate this into Swedish!
Att förvandla vatten till vin.	To change water into wine.
Hon har rest ut på (till) landet.	She has gone into the country.

Of (Cf. §§ 48—54)

Är ni rädd **för** hunden?	Are you afraid of the dog?
Det skulle aldrig falla mig in. (Jag skulle inte drömma **om** en sådan sak.)	I should not dream of such a thing.
Han har en hög tanke **om** sin överste.	He thinks a lot of his colonel.
Han har berövat mig mina pengar.	He has robbed me *of* my money.
Han anklagades **för** stöld.	He was accused of theft.
En karta **över** England.	A map of England.
Drottningen av England.	The Queen of England.
Konungariket Sverige.	The kingdom *of* Sweden.
Staden Stockholm.	The city *of* Stockholm.

191

Ett kilo socker.	Two pounds *of* sugar.
En liter mjölk.	Two pints *of* milk.
Bergets fot. (Cf. §§ 45—46.)	The foot of the mountain.
Bordsbenen.	The legs of the table.
Stockholms universitet.	The University of Stockholm.
Uppsala[1] universitet.	The University of Uppsala.
Han är en god vän **till mig.**	He is an old friend *of mine.*
I norra Sverige.	In the north *of* Sweden.
Uppsala ligger norr **om** Stockholm.	Uppsala is situated to the north of Stockholm.
Vi var fyra stycken.	There were four of us.

To

Skall ni resa **till** Sverige nästa sommar?	Are you going to Sweden next summer?
Han har alltid varit mycket vänlig **mot** mig.	He has always been very kind to me.
Får jag presentera er **för** herr Bergman.	May I introduce you to Mr. Bergman.
Kan jag få tala **med** herr Andersson?	May I speak to Mr. Andersson?
Tio **mot** en (ett).	Ten to one.
Han tog inte av sig hatten **för** mig.	He did not take off his hat to me.
(Det är svårt **att** veta.	It is difficult to know.)

314 [EXAMPLES ILLUSTRATING THE USE OF CERTAIN SWEDISH PREPOSITIONS

Över

Staden ligger 100 meter **över** havsytan.	The town is situated 300 feet *above* sea-level.
Klockan är **över** elva.	It is *past* eleven o'clock.
Han gick **över** gatan.	He crossed the street.
Han gick **tvärs över** parken.	He walked *across* the park.

---

[1] An old genitive without the **-s** ending.

192

Reste ni **över** Göteborg?	Did you go *by* Gothenburg?
Det går **över** min horisont.	That is *beyond* me.
Vad beklagar ni er **över?**	What are you complaining *of?*

Under

Katten är **under** bordet.	The cat is *under* the table.
Det är tio grader **under** noll.	It is ten degrees *below* zero.
Levnadskostnaderna var mycket höga **under** kriget.	The cost of living was very high *during* the war.
Under hans regering.	*In* (During) his reign.
Under tiden.	*In* the meantime.

Om; omkring

Han vek **om** hörnet.	He turned /round/ the corner.
En föreläsning **om** Sverige.	A lecture *on* Sweden.
Vad talar han **om?**	What is he talking *about?*
Norr **om** Stockholm.	North (To the north) *of* Stockholm.
De seglade **om** oss.	They sailed *past* us.
Om dagen. **Om** natten.	*In* the daytime. *At* night.
Om morgnarna. **Om** onsdagarna.	*In* the morning/s/. *On* Wednesdays.
Jag kommer tillbaka **om** en vecka (**om** en liten stund).	I shall be back *in* a week's time (*in* a little while).
Han reser bort en gång **om** året.	He goes away once *a* year.
Två gånger **om** dagen.[1]	Twice *a* day.
Kommer ni **om** (*or:* nästa) onsdag?	Are you coming next Wednesday?
Tiggaren bad **om** en bit bröd.	The beggar asked *for* a piece of bread.
Vad frågade han er **om?**	What did he ask you *about?*
Vi dansade **omkring** majstången.	We danced *round* the maypole.
Omkring hundra personer.	*About* a hundred people.
Hon såg sig **om/kring/.**	She looked about her (looked round).

---

[1] But: *två gånger* **i** *veckan* (**i** *månaden*).

Word-order

315 POSITION OF THE SUBJECT

The Subject is generally placed before the Verb in declarative sentences. There are, however, many exceptions. They are treated in § 316.

316 In principal clauses the Subject is placed *after* the (finite) Verb (**inverted word-order**) in the following cases:

(*a*) In Interrogative Sentences where the Subject is not an Interrogative Pronoun.

Talar er fru svenska?	Does your wife speak Swedish?
Går ni redan?	Are you going already?
Har han inte gått ännu?	Has he not gone yet?

(*b*) When the Sentence begins with the Object, a Predicative Noun or a Predicative Adjective.

Vad **gör ni** om söndagarna?	What do you do with yourself on Sundays?
Den här boken **har min far köpt** i London.	This book my father has bought in London.
Det **har jag** aldrig **hört.**	I never heard that.
Till professor i engelska **utnämndes Dr William Smith.**	Dr William Smith was appointed Professor of English.
Vackert **kan man** inte kalla det.	You cannot call it beautiful.

(*c*) When the Sentence begins with an Adverb or with an Adverbial Phrase.

Nu **är våren** här.	Now spring is here.
Sedan **gick vargen** tillbaka till skogen.	Then the wolf went back to the wood.
Om somrarna **bor vi** på landet.	In summer we live in the country.

I går **var det** mycket kallt.	Yesterday it was very cold.
I dag **är det** varmt.	Today it is warm.
Vart **tog kniven** vägen?	What became of the knife?
När **går tåget?**	When does the train start?
Om en timme **kommer** brevbäraren.	In an hour the postman will be here.

(d) In a Principal Clause when it is preceded by a Subordinate Clause.

När vedhuggaren hade tappat sin yxa, **visste han** inte, vad han skulle ta sig till.	When the wood-cutter had lost his axe, he did not know what to do.
Om du inte är där senast klockan sju, **väntar jag** inte på dig.	If you are not there by seven o'clock at the latest, I shall not wait for you.

(e) In the Principal Clause after a Direct Quotation.

»Hur står det till?» **frågade han.**	"How are you?" he asked.
»Tack, bra», **svarade hon.**	"Quite well, thanks," she answered.

(f) Often in Optative Clauses (expressing a wish).

Tillkomme ditt rike.	Thy kingdom come.
Leve konungen!	Long live the King!

NOTE. — (a) Subordinate Clauses have, as a rule, normal (uninverted) word-order.

Jag vet inte, vad **han har** gjort.	I don't know what he has done.

NOTE. — (b) The inverted word-order is used in Conditional Clauses where the conjunction om 'if' is omitted.

Vore jag som du, så svarade jag inte.	If I were you, I should not answer.

Kommer han hit, så skall jag
tala om det för honom.

If he comes here, I will tell him.

POSITION OF THE OBJECT

317 The Indirect Object, when used without any Preposition, precedes
the Direct Object.

Ge **honom den**!

Give it him!

Han lovade att skicka **mig det.**

He promised to send it me.

POSITION OF THE ADVERB

318 (*a*) **In Principal Clauses**

In Principal Clauses the Adverb is placed *after* the Verb (in
compound tenses immediately after the Auxiliary Verb).

Det **glömde** jag **alldeles** bort.	I quite forgot.
Han **går nästan aldrig** ut och går.	He hardly ever goes for a walk.
Hon **tänkte aldrig** på det.	She never thought of it.
Han **gick snart.**	He soon left.
Hon **insåg då,** att det var för sent.	She then realized that it was too late.
Jag **träffade en gång** en kusin till er.	I once met a cousin of yours.
Hon **undvek omsorgsfullt** att se på mig.	She carefully avoided looking at me.
Jag **trodde nästan,** att han var död.	I almost thought he was dead.
Han **vägrade visligen** att gå.	He wisely refused to go.
Han **kommer ofta** hit.	He often comes here.
Han **reser alltid** till södra Frankrike om vintrarna.	He always goes to the south of France in winter.

Han **kom snart** underfund med det.	He soon found it out.
Han minns det **än.**	He still remembers it.
Lämna aldrig dörren olåst!	Never leave the door unlocked!
Jag **har aldrig träffat** honom.	I have never met him.

(b) In Subordinate Clauses 319

In Subordinate Clauses many Adverbs are placed *before* the Verb (in compound tenses before the Auxiliary Verb), e. g. *icke, inte, ej, ingalunda, bara, aldrig, alltid, ofta, snart, sällan, antagligen, förmodligen, möjligen, vanligen, visserligen, gärna, just.*

Jag visste, att han **inte hade** varit där.	I knew that he *had not* been there.
De, som **inte är** färdiga i tid, får stanna hemma.	Those who *are not* ready in time must stay at home.
Det är en melodi, som man **ofta hör.**	It is a tune that one often hears.
Värden, som **bara kunde** tala tyska, svarade inte.	The landlord, who *could only* speak German, did not reply.
Han sade, att han **snart skulle** komma tillbaka.	He said he *would soon* be back.
Det hade varit bättre, om han **aldrig hade** kommit.	It would have been better if he *had never* come.
Det var något, som jag **omöjligen kunde** veta.	It was something I *could not possibly* know.
Jag medgav, att han **antagligen hade** rätt.	I admitted that he was probably right.
Det berättas, att **han** på denna resa **för första gången fick se** negerslavar i arbete.[1]	It is related that on this journey *he saw, for the first time,* negro slaves at work.

---

[1] Note the Swedish word-order: the adverbials are placed between the subject *(han)* and the verb.

320 Demonstrative Adverbs, and Adverbs expressing a (more or less) definite time, place or manner are placed after the Verb (as in English).

Jag vet, att han bor **här.** I know that he lives here.

Om han reser i dag, /så/ kommer If he leaves today he will be han fram **om fredag.** there on Friday.

Han arbetar långsamt men sä- He works slowly but surely. kert.

321 The Adverbs *icke, inte, ej, alltid,* and *aldrig* are placed **between** *att* and the Infinitive. Other Adverbs may either be placed between *att* and the Infinitive, or **after** the Infinitive (not before *att*).

Jag bönföll honom **att inte göra** I implored him *not to do* it. det.

Han lovade **att aldrig göra** om He promised never to do it again. det.

Att alltid förlåta är bättre än Always to forgive is better than **att aldrig förlåta.** never to forgive.

Han fick order **att genast läm-** He was ordered to leave the **na** landet. country immediately.

USE OF CAPITAL LETTERS

322 Names of **countries** are spelt with capital letters; but not nouns and adjectives denoting nationality and languages. E. g.:

Han är engelsman. Han talar engelska, tyska och franska. Sverige och svenskarna. Är ni svensk? Förstår ni svenska? En svensk för-fattare ('author'). Jag känner många norrmän och danskar ('I know many Norwegians and Danes').

323 Names of **places** are spelt with capital letters; but not nouns and adjectives derived from such names. E. g.:

Han är stockholmare. Det stockholmska uttalet av bokstaven 'ä'. Han är gift med en parisiska ('He is married to a Parisian lady').

198

Names of **months, days** of the week and church **festivals** are spelt 324
with small letters. E. g.:

Första måndagen i augusti. Dagen före juldagen kallas julafton.
Dagen efter påsksöndagen kallas annandag påsk ('Easter Monday').

Titles used with names are written with small letters.[1] E. g.: 325

Jag har skrivit till professor Lund, greve ('Count') Bonde, överste
('Colonel') Kjellman och ingenjör Eriksson. Jag mötte prins Carl
och prinsessan Ingeborg.

Similarly:

ag bor hos farbror ('Uncle') Fredrik och faster ('Aunt') Emma.
Karl den store ('Charlemagne'). Oscar den andre.

Nouns and adjectives denoting **religion, political parties,** etc., 326
are written with small letters. E. g.:

Hon är katolik. Han är socialdemokrat. Det liberala partiet. Han är
riksdagsman ('a Member of Parliament').

PUNCTUATION

The **comma** is used to separate dependent clauses from main clauses. 327
Note especially the use of the comma before the conjunction *att* and
before a relative clause. E. g.:

Jag visste, att han hade gjort det. Han visade mig kameran, som han
hade köpt i Göteborg. Hon kom, när jag gick därifrån. Han frågade,
om hon var sjuk.

EXCEPTION: No comma is used before *att* when it is governed by a
preposition; nor before a relative clause when the relative pronoun
is omitted. E. g.:

Hon beklagade sig över att hon inte hade fått någon biljett. Tåget
han skulle resa med hade redan gått.

---

[1] Except when used as terms of address in letters, etc., e. g. *Herr Professor! Bästa
Fru Björkman!*

328 The **colon** is used before a direct quotation (corresponding to English comma), e. g.:

När jag reste, sa min mamma: »Glöm inte att skriva, när du kommer fram!»

329 The **exclamation mark** has a wider use than in English. It is used after imperatives and words of caution, e. g. *Märk! Obs.!* (both meaning 'Note'; 'N. B.'). Also after the words of address at the beginning of a letter (corresponding to English comma). E. g.:

Kära vänner! Bästa Fru Andersson! Herr Professor!

330 The **apostrophe** is not used before the genitival **-s;** but it is used to mark the genitive of a noun ending in **-s** or **-z.** E. g.:

Klas' kamrater. Creutz' närmaste vänner.